Under the Shadow of Death

Newest Other Titles From Pyramid Press

A Time of War
By Michael Peterson

Shike Time of The Dragons
By Robert Shea

Shike Last of The Zinja
By Robert Shea

The Eighth Plague
By Kyle C. Fitzharris

Under The Shadow of Death
By Garabed Hagop Aaronian (Aharonian)

Under the Shadow of Death

MEMOIRS OF A SURVIVOR OF THE ARMENIAN GENOCIDE

By
Garabed Hagop Aaronian (Aharonian)

PYRAMID PRESS

Copyright ©2014 James Aaronian

All rights reserved. No part of this book, in part or in whole, may be reproduced, transmitted, or utilized, in any form or by any means, electronic or mechanical, including photocopying, recording, or by any information storage and retrieval system, without permission in writing from the publisher, except for brief quotations in critical articles, books and reviews.

International Standard Book Number: 10: 0989901750
International Standard Book Number: 13: 978-0-9899017-5-8

First Pyramid Press Edition 2014

The paper used in this publication meets the minimum requirements of the American National Standard for Permanence of Paper for Printed Library Materials Z39.48-1984.
Printed in U.S.A.

PYRAMID PRESS
9550 South Eastern Avenue • Suite 253
Las Vegas, NV 89123 U.S.A.
contact@pyramidpress.net

Acknowledgments

A special note of appreciation is extended to:

Armen Aroyan for his time and expertise in editing this manuscript as well as providing some of the recent photographs;

Cousin Sharon Saroyan who painstakingly and lovingly typed a version of this manuscript years ago.

You have made this book possible and our sincere thanks are extended to you.

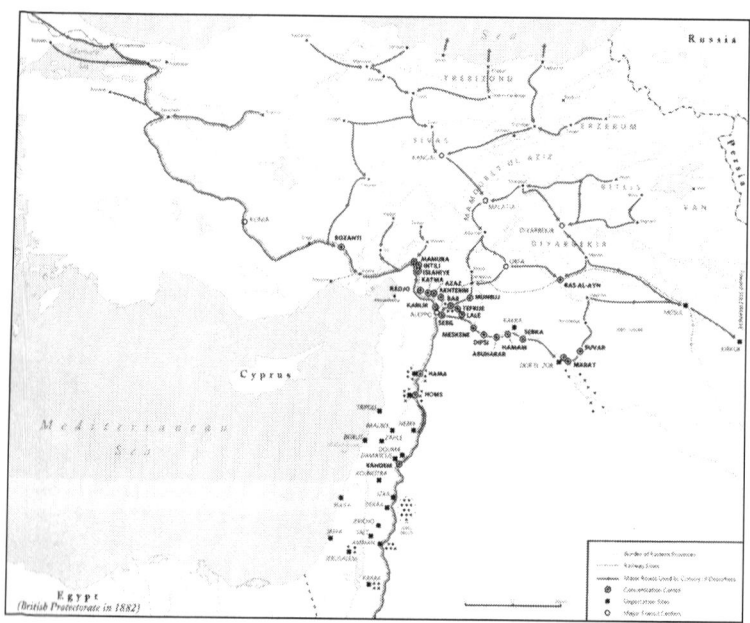

Map showing the border of eastern provinces, railway lines, major roads used by convoy of deportees, concentration camps, deportation sites and major transit centers.

A convoy of refugees on the road toward Sivas.

Table of Contents

Preface		xi
1	My Birthplace	1
2	Massacres Of Sultan Abdul Hamid	5
3	The "Uncle"	13
4	The Medresseh And The Mice	17
5	Deceived	21
6	My Mother And Father	23
7	The Dervish And My Uncle	27
8	My Cousin "Arab"	31
9	The Lie	35
10	Liberty, Equality, And Fraternity	41
11	Ali Effendi, The Ulema	45
12	The Balkan War And The Volunteers	51
13	Against My Will, I Became A Leader	57
14	Burhan Bey, The Gentleman	65
15	The Beginning Of The Tempest	69
16	The Hollow Pit	73
17	Great Is The Power Of Christ	75
18	The End Of Lebanese Autonomy	77
19	Caravans Of Exiles	79
20	The Supreme Head Of The Armenian Church	81
21	In Aleppo	83
22	My Mother And Sister	87
23	Fatih's Mistake	91

Continued

In the fall of 1915, Armenian refugees in the street in Aleppo.

Table of Contents

24	On The Amanos Mountains	95
25	How I Became A "Yaver"	101
26	Akiah Bey	105
27	Caravans Of The Deported	109
28	The Donkey–The Only Friend	113
29	The Cache	117
30	The Bride	119
31	The Bandit Leader And His Dagger	123
32	The Two Lovers	127
33	Chief Of The Code	131
34	To Be Or Not To Be A Mohammedan	137
35	My Sister Alice	141
36	The Last Goodbye	143
37	Twenty-Four Hours	147
38	The Helpful Germans	155
38	I Tore Down A Church	157
40	Scratch The Turk and You Find The Tartar	161
41	My Sister Alice, Again	169
42	Magnanimous Bulgars	171
43	Men or Mice	175
44	In The Land of Four Freedoms	177
Eulogy		181

On November 2, 1895, after the massacres in Erzurum, victims were buried in the Armenian cemetary.

Preface

The land situated around Mount Ararat was a paradise at one time. The natives of that land, the Armenians, a peaceful and God-fearing people, were toiling and tilling the earth and "In the sweat of their faces they ate their bread."

They were "fruitful and multiplied," and tried to replenish the earth according to God's command. But they neglected a very important part of God's command—"to subdue it" and protect it from invaders.

The Turks invaded that Paradise and turned it into a Jehennem (hell, or a place of suffering), and the Armenians suffered and were annihilated, one million of them.

In my hometown as a teacher, in the Turkish Engineering School in Constantinople, as a student and in the Turkish Army as an Engineer-Officer, I lived with and among them. I saw the Turk as a gentleman and I knew him as a blood thirsty beast.

This is the story of the gentleman and the beast.

It is the truth, the whole truth, and nothing but the truth, and may God have mercy upon the souls of those innocent people, my people, who suffered and died, many not even given the dignity of a grave.

Lest their memory be forgotten by those who escaped the Jehennem, and for the generations to come, LET THIS BE A REMINDER.

Garabed Hagop Aaronian (Aharonian)

1

My Birthplace

The day was Thursday, I remember it well, the month of October 1895. I was a little child sitting in front of our window and watching the vast plain that was spreading far and wide, surrounded by high mountain ranges. Scattered all over the plain were little villages, hundreds of them, so near each other that the villagers with powerful voices could converse across the plain.

Some of the villages belonged to Armenians, some to Turks, and some to both. Some of them were almost lost in trees, and all one could see was a cluster of green leaves. Some of them, on the contrary, had no trees at all, and one could plainly see all the huts built of mud bricks.

"My son," my father used to remark, "those villages which are buried amongst the trees and are surrounded with vineyards belong to the Armenians. They are peaceful, hardworking people. They are not afraid of work, and as the saying goes, they can extract bread out of rocks. The other villages that are void of trees, vineyards, and fields, belong to the Turks. They are lazy, good-for-nothing people. They hate work. That is the reason that Armenians everywhere are prosperous and well-to-do, while Turks are poor and half-starved all the time. That is the reason they are always jealous of the Armenians, and hate them so. They want to kill us, rob us, and take away from us what we have earned by our sweat. Although they have the government, the power—and theirs is the country—yet we own the fields, the vineyards, the houses, the trade, and the wealth."

"Look," my father would conclude, "look, even in those villages which are inhabited both by Armenians and Turks, you can easily detect the Armenian and Turkish Quarters just by looking at the trees and the vineyards. Armenian Quarters are always surrounded with trees and orchards."

Our village was situated at the foot of the northern mountain range and extended partly over the plain. Our house was built at the highest spot of the village, between Gregorian and Protestant Churches. It is an old Armenian custom to build their churches at the highest spot of the village. They build them with white cut stones, beautiful, magnificent, and dominant, with a high dome at the center and a huge cross on its top.

From far away one could always see the churches dominating the villages, their crosses shining in the sun. Villagers, working in the fields, morning and evening, would gaze at these pillars of life and cross their hearts. The churches were the pride of the villagers. They themselves would live in small houses, in mud huts, but they would build big, magnificent churches, so that on Sunday morning they could attend the solemn high mass together. The churches were the manifestation of their faith, deep was the foundation of these churches, solid were their walls, and exalted as the crosses on their domes.

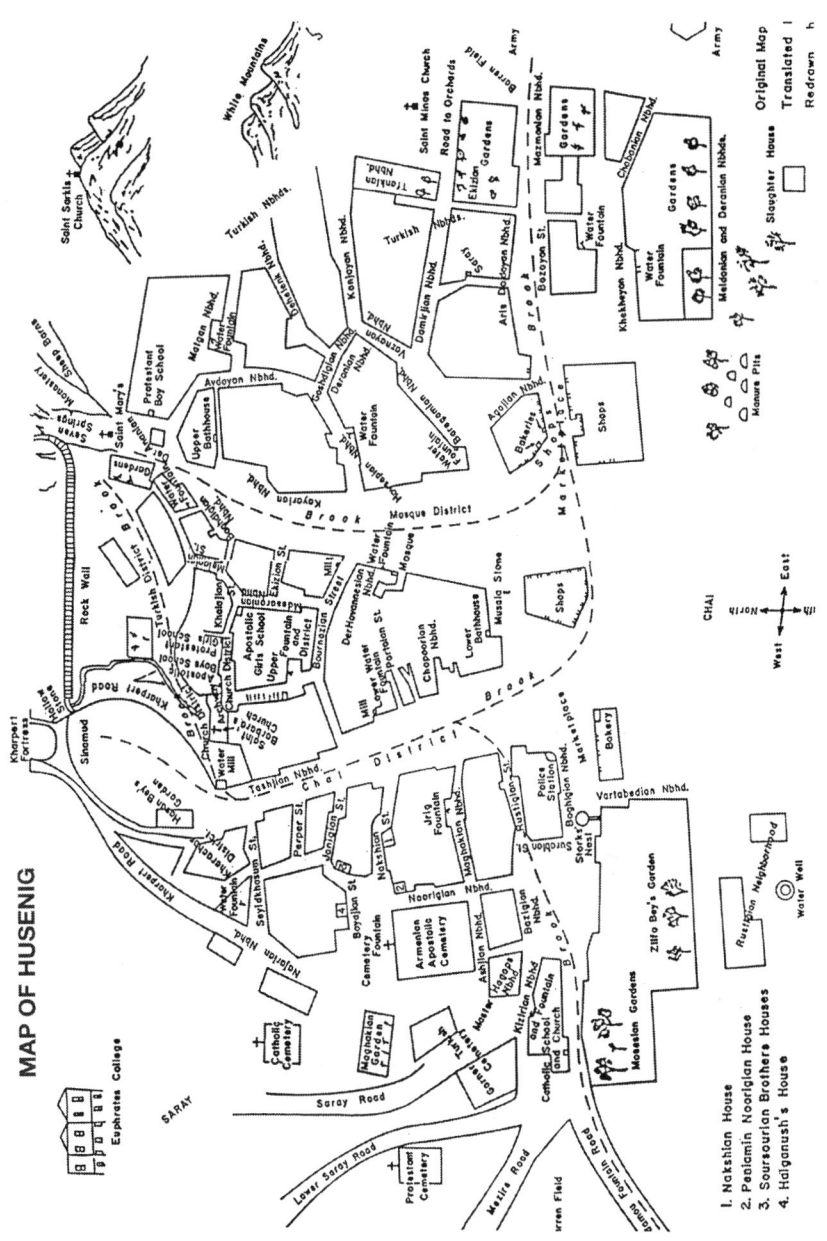

Village of Husenik

2

The Massacres Of Sultan Abdul Hamid

The day was Thursday, as I said before, and I was sitting in front of our window, watching the villages on the plain. Suddenly I noticed a huge cloud of smoke emerging from the Armenian village, "Tlgadin," (Kuylu) which was ten miles away from our village. It was not the ordinary pattern of smoke, narrow and tall like poplar trees, which was pouring out of a chimney. It was wide, thick, black as pitch, engulfing the entire village.

I called to my father. Father hadn't gone to work that day, and he was helping Mother fill the secret cave of our house with bedding, clothing, kitchenware, and food.

Father came to the window, gave one look and said, "The Turks are massacring, plundering. They have poured kerosene over the houses and are burning them. Poor Tlgadin Armenians."

Father sighed, lifted his eyes to the heavens, his lips were moving. Praying or cursing—maybe both. I could see tears in his eyes. He slowly returned to his work in the cave.

I was nine years old. I could see and I could hear, but I could not understand. I had not the slightest realization of what my father meant.

The next day was Friday. I was again at my window, watching the villages in the plain. The same thick, black smoke started rising up from another village, "Khirkhrig". This time I did not call my father—I knew the answer. They were massacring, plundering and burning "Khirkhrig."

My father was already closing the entrance of the cave with brick and mortar.

The night came, we spread our mattresses on the floor and lay down to sleep—five brothers and a baby sister.

Father and Mother could not sleep, although they were tired. They were whispering and there was anxiety in their voices. I could hear, but I could not understand. I could not visualize the menace that was hanging over our heads.

Saturday it was the turn of "Kesrig" a village only three miles away from our home. Again the black, thick smoke poured into the night sky.

Father and Mother had built a fire in front of the closed cave entrance to make the mortar dry and look like the rest of the wall.

The school teacher, Baron Dikran, walked into our house with a broad smile on his face. "Hagop aghbar, cheer up," he addressed my father. "I have very reliable and good news to give to you. Keri (nickname for the Russians, meaning uncle) is already at the river near Palu, and is going to be here Monday morning."

My father could scarcely read or write, but he did not believe the teacher who could read and write. My father did not believe him because he, being a butcher by trade, had traveled far and wide among the tribesmen, living on the mountain ranges along the Turkish and Russian borders, to buy sheep and goats. He knew very well that it would take a fortnight for a horseman to travel the distance that was separating the Russian border from the Palu River. As for the Russian Army, it would take months against the Turkish Army, fortified cities, mountains, river, and narrow passes.

"Baron Dikran," my father said, "you have believed it yourself, but do not try to make the others believe it and slumber in pleasant dreams. My own Turkish friends have already informed me that our day of massacre and plunder is on Monday. Can't you see the smoke that is coming up from the villages one after the other, and like a prairie fire is devouring everything and coming nearer and nearer to our village? Monday is our turn to be massacred, plundered, and our houses burned to ashes. There can be no Keri at the bank of the Palu River. It is impossible."

I was too young to know who was right and who was wrong. I was only wishing and praying that in spite of my father's pessimistic judgment, Baron Dikran, the teacher, was right and that "Keree," our "Russian uncle," would be in our village to save us from the Turks and their massacres.

It was Sunday morning. It was the turn of "Morenig," a little village only one mile away from our village, going up in smoke. Sitting in front of our window I could clearly see the smoke of kerosene, with the flames licking into the air.

My father, with the help of Mother and my elder brother, was moving the empty petaks (big earthen jars) in front of the closed entrance of the cave.

At noontime, Hamdi Chavush, a Turk friend of my father and uncles, came and invited us to his home for shelter and protection. We shouldered every bedding and all the food we could carry and moved into his home.

The house was big, but it was not big enough to shelter four extra families, therefore, we and my uncle's family moved next door into his sister's house. His sister was a widow with one son, Ali. Although the house was small, fourteen of us managed to squeeze ourselves into one room. Monday morning, just before the sunrise, the trumpeter from the top of the hill, "Saint Sarkis," started blowing his trumpet. He was ordering the Turkish and Kurdish mob, gathered on the outskirts of the village, to attack.

"Allah, Allah, Bism Allah" (in the name of Allah). We clearly heard the shouts, and through the cracks of the door my father and uncle could see the frenzied crowds with their guns, sabers, swords, daggers and yatagans, pouring through the narrow streets to kill the Armenians, to plunder and burn their homes.

Hamdi Chavush was standing on the top of the flat roof of his house, holding his shotgun in his hand. We could hear him hollering to the frenzied mob. "This street is inhabited by Turks, do not harm anybody. Go to the central section of the village, which belongs to the Armenians."

It was the order of Sultan Abdul Hamid that the Armenians should be massacred. Hamdi Chavush, single-handed, could not go against that order, but he was trying to save us—his Armenian friends. He stood all day on that flat roof, gun in hand, and guarded us in his house and his sister's house. He did not kill. He did not plunder.

We could distinctly hear, in the central part of the village, the guns barking, the Turkish and Kurdish mobs shouting "Allah, Allah," and the Armenians screaming, crying, trying to reach the safety of the hills, and many dying.

Three hours later, the trumpeter on top of the hill once again sounded the trumpet, and the murderers and plunderers stopped their sinister mission.

Hamdi Chavush sent us word that the danger had passed.

Tuesday, my father and uncle went out to look over the village. One hour later they returned and informed us that everything in our house was plundered, but thank God, they had not found our secret cave.

Our cache was safe, but my mother's sister and her son, Vahan, a thirteen-year old boy, were massacred. They had laid down my cousin, Vahan, and cut his throat. My aunt, his mother, had tried to protect him, but in vain. They had split her head with a blow of an axe.

My father said, "They, mother and son were lying on the ground side by side, Vahan's throat cut and my sister-in-law's brain poured out, and their blood pooled around them"

My mother was crying silently. She could not scream for fear the neighboring Turks would hear. She suffered silently.

My father and uncle had white turbans wrapped around their fezes. They had become Mohammedans. That was the order. Any Armenian who didn't want to be slaughtered had to deny his Christian faith and become Mohammedan. My father and uncle and all the Armenians had denied their Christian faith and overnight had accepted the Mohammedan faith. What could they do? Life is so dear. They did not want to be slaughtered.

Wednesday, we returned home. Every room was empty. The Turks and Kurds had done a clean job. Every piece of furniture, kitchenware, bedding, and every bit of food was carried away. Anything they could not carry had been broken with an axe or hammer.

They had broken the earthen jars containing cereal, flour, grape juice sweets, dried mulberries and scattered them over the floor. Then they had broken the jug of vinegar and poured it over them so we would not be able to eat them.

In spite of all that, we were lucky, lucky indeed, compared with the other unfortunate Armenians. The plunderers had not found our cache.

Father and brother pushed aside the petaks, (bee hives) covering the cache entrance, tore down the wall closing the entrance, and we had enough food, clothing, and bedding to live on during the winter.

In our part of the country we did not have grocery stores. People stored everything after the harvest, enough for one year. They stored the wheat, the flour, the shredded wheat, grape juice, dried mulberries, wine, and dry vegetables. They killed lamb, cut it into small pieces, fried it in fat, and stored it. Along the walls of their cellars, you could see the big pot bellied jugs, four feet high, standing in rows, all filled with provisions.

Armenian ministers and priests—white turbans around their fezes—had buried the massacred 118 men, women, and children. 118 men, women and babies out of a population of 4000 villagers. Not a large portion thanks to many Turks like Hamdi Chavush, that had sheltered and protected their Armenian friends. At the first sound of the trumpet, they had opened their homes and invited the escaping Armenians, friends or no friends, into the protection of their homes.

The nearby hills, the caves, the rocks, the vineyards had sheltered the rest.

Yes, the Turks are not all killers—they are not all plunderers. Many were peaceful, friendly and good-hearted. But it is sad and unfortunate, that the Turks for six hundred years, being a warrior nation, have been forced to take orders, to obey their superiors, their princes, pashas, sultans, and priests. Once those superiors give the order, the plunderers, the killers, the hoodlums, their cohorts, and the priests would gain control and perform their criminal and heinous deeds.

On every Armenian's front door they glued a small piece of paper with these words on it, LA-I-LA-HA-IL-ALLAH. (there is no god but Allah, and Mohammed his prophet). We had become Mohammedans.

Turkish dignitaries came to our church to decide on the location of the Minaret. They were planning to change our beautiful church into a mosque. Why not? Are we not all Mohammedans now.

My elder brother, Apel, fourteen years old, had to leave school to help Father in his butcher's business. With the few Turkish pounds that were in my father's purse, they bought sheep, took them to the slaughter house in the early, cold, wintry mornings. When the blizzard blew the temperature dropped to thirty below zero. The whole country gets blanketed, knee deep with snow and ice, and icicles hung down from men's mustaches.

It was a miserable life for Father, and especially for Brother—so young was he. But they had to endure it, because there were six other mouths to be fed besides their own.

3

The "Uncle"

Baron Dikran was wrong. "Uncle" did not come to our help on Monday when 118 people had been killed.

We buried our dead on Wednesday, "Uncle" did not show up. The Turks had broken the gates of the church with axes, the iron bars on the windows were all broken and twisted, the altar was in ruins, the church was pilfered. The rugs, the silverware, the gold and silver covered crosses, and the Bibles were all carried away.

They did not repair the gate, the windows, nor the altar, because they hoped "Uncle," or at least his emissaries would come to witness the cruelties, the ruins, the graves, the sufferings that the Armenians, the Christians had suffered at the hands of the Turks, the Mohammedans.

"Uncle"—this one word that I heard for the first time from Baron Dikran when I was nine years old, am still hearing now, when I am an old man. "Uncle"—in that single word is enveloped a great part of Armenian tragedy.

For one hundred and fifty years, six generations of Armenians hoped fervently that our northern neighbor, our "Christian neighbor," Russia, would heed the pleas and recognize sufferings, tortures, the massacres of this little Christian nation, invade Turkey, occupy the old historical Armenia, now under Turkish rule, liberate it from Turkish yoke, and make them free so they could worship their God, their Christ in peace. For six generations they hoped and prayed for that day of liberation.

Russia, every twenty-five years since 1815, in order to obtain a warm port over warm water waged war with Turkey to occupy its country and reach the Mediterranean Sea. Each time the Armenians thought the day of liberation was at hand, the Christian "Uncle" was pushed back from Turkish territory with the help of this or that Christian nation. The Christian Armenians could not grasp nor understand why any Christian nation would help a Mohammedan nation against another Christian nation that was about to liberate them.

Their ancestors, fifteen hundred years ago, could not grasp why, at the time they were fighting the Zoroastrian sun worshippers (the Persians) for their Christian faith, and willingly dying for Christ, the Christian Greeks would not help them in their fight.

Christianity with Armenians was their body and soul, their whole existence, their nationality. "Armenianity" was the label on the bottle whose content was Christianity. ANY ARMENIAN WHO WAS NOT CHRISTIAN WAS NOT AN ARMENIAN—THAT WAS THEIR CREED.

This is unique only for Armenians. A Frenchman becomes an Islam, but he is still a Frenchman. An Englishman may become a Buddhist and still remain an Englishman, but an Armenian Islam, or an Armenian Buddhist, or an Armenian fire worshipper is no longer an Armenian. He is a Persian, a Hindu, a Turk, as the case may be, but never an Armenian.

The Armenian nation throws out that "infidel," that "unbeliever," that "traitor," that "denier," from its main body, as the ocean throws the dead fish from its waters. An Armenian is a Christian, nothing but a Christian. "A Non-Christian Armenian" the Armenian mind did not grasp 1500 years ago and cannot grasp it today.

A small nation, surrounded by heathens, fire worshippers, Mohammedans, over-run by them, but still keeping their faith. They suffered, were plundered and massacred, but they kept their faith and hoped.

They hoped that other Christian nations would come and help them, would liberate them. They even asked for their assistance, for their intervention and help. They believed in those nations—thinking that those nations' Christianity and faith were as strong, genuine, and deep-rooted as theirs. And the result was that the Turks became more irritated and doubled, tripled their persecutions of the Armenians.

The Armenian Christian's mind did not grasp it, and they prayed, waited and hoped. The help did not come, the oppression became more severe and the sufferings more unbearable. The Armenians' hopes turned to curses—curses against the Christian nations that had forsaken them, nations that were deaf to their cries, nations refusing to help them. To their emotional suffering minds, all the Christian powers became canards, cheaters, liars, selfish and evil-minded.

For one hundred-fifty years they prayed for the success of the Russian Army. In World War One their sympathy was with the allies. They volunteered in the French Legion and in the Russian Armies, and the result was EXTERMINATION INSTEAD OF LIBERATION. They did not understand why Christian nations were fighting among themselves and the Mohammedans standing by were watching them kill each other on the shores of Africa.

The Armenians, in the Middle Ages, sided with the Crusaders. They sided with every movement, every war that was Christian against Mohammedan, and at the end they were disappointed. They did not understand that there is no Christianity in power politics. There is no Christianity in a nation's struggle for it's economical supremacy.

To this day, that same Christian-Armenian nation, that incurable nation, is waiting emotionally and instinctively, hoping and wishing for "Keri" to invade Turkey, occupy historic Armenian territory under Turkish domination, liberate it, and turn it over to the Armenians.

4

The Medresseh And The Mice

We, the entire village folks, had become Mohammedans. Our schools, our churches were all closed.

My father could scarcely read or write, but he did not want his children to be illiterate. One morning he took me and my brother Krikor, who was a couple of years older than I, to the Medresseh (Turkish School). The school was one small room attached to the mosque. Along the three sides of the room, three feet away from the walls, there was an upright board about two feet high with a nine inch slanted board nailed to it. The pupils were kneeling side by side in close quarters behind this bookstand, had placed their books over the slanted board and were reading aloud in monotone, swinging their bodies back and forth to the rhythm of the monotone.

The teacher, a very old man, with a white trimmed beard and mustache, and a large white turban around his fez was squatting on a little mat near the door.

"Selamen Aleykum, Hodja Effendi," my father saluted.

"Aleykum Selam," Hodja responded.

"Here, I brought my two sons to your school and I am leaving them in your care. If they do not behave nor try to learn, let their flesh be yours and their skins and bones mine."

This last expression meant that Hodja was free to beat us as much as he pleased.

"Don't worry, I will do my best," answered Hodja Effendi.

"Allaha Ismarladik," said my father, and left the school.

Hodja made us sit at the end of the row near the door. He assigned one of the older pupils to be our "Kalfa" or (tutor). We began to learn the Arabic alphabet. There were no grades in the school—everybody was for himself. The goal of the school was to teach the pupils to read and memorize. The sooner one accomplished this, the sooner he graduated from the school.

If you thought you had learned your lesson, you would kneel in front of the Hodja and read it. When Hodja was satisfied, he would assign you another lesson. You could repeat this in one day as many times as you wished, as few times as you wished, or not at all.

If you wanted to leave the room, you did not have to get permission from Hodja. There was a small board, a little larger than a hand, hanging from the wall on a string. On one side of the board was written "OUT," on the other side, "IN." One would turn the board "OUT" and walk out, but if the board was already showing "OUT" all the others had to wait until the other pupil returned and turned the board "IN."

There were two methods of punishment. If one's guilt was a small one, one of the Kalfas would get up, and with his arms, he would hold the guilty one's shoulders tightly and turn his back to Hodja. Hodja would hit him on his back with a stick until another one of the Kalfas would get up, stand between Hodja and the pupil's back and say "Affediniz (pardon him), Hodja effendi." Hodja would say, "I pardon him," and stop beating him.

If one had a Kalfa friend, the punishment would be one or two strokes, because the friend would interfere right away. But if one did not have a friend, God help him, because Hodja would not stop until his arm became tired, or the stick broke. That depended on one's luck.

The second punishment was the falaka for a more severe guilt. The guilty one would lie down on his back on the floor and lift his bare feet. Two of the Kalfae would bring the falaka, which was a yard long stick with a heavy rope attached to both ends. They passed his feet between the rope and the stick and wrapped the rope around the stick. Two Kalfas standing on either side of him held the ends of the stick and Hodja would start beating the guilty one's soles of his feet as hard as he could with a stick. He would not stop hitting him until another Kalfa would stand between the feet and Hodja's stick and ask his pardon with the customary expression "Affediniz Hodja effendi."

It was on the third day that we were in school when we noticed that the area under the wooden floor that we were sitting on was infested with mice. They were so bold and unafraid that they came out of their hiding place and tried to nibble on our little lunches. These lunches usually consisted of bread and a small piece of white cheese, the size of two forefingers. We could not stand the filth of the mice. No Armenian could stand this filth but the Turks had lived in this squalor for years, since the days when the mosque and the school were built. They did not know any better.

We asked Hodja if we could exterminate them. Hodja was more than glad to have us do it. We ran home, got two of the mousetraps that were lying idle in our house—one of the few things that the Turks and the Kurds had not carried away. We brought them to school, set them up and pushed them under the floor through the holes in the floor. One minute later—chuck, chuck,—two traps, two mice.

"Carry them out," was Hodja's order. We did so.

We set them again. One more minute, and again—chuck, chuck,—two more mice. This operation continued until it was time for school to close, and by that time we had exterminated thirty-four of them. The place was still full of them, and they were all so hungry. We continued our exterminating process for several days, but day after day our bagging became smaller and smaller. It was on the seventh day that we did not catch any mice.

We were satisfied and happy. Hodja was also happy, and he gave us a handful of raisins. They tasted so sweet and delicious.

The Turks had carried away our raisins and my father couldn't afford to buy them again.

5

Deceived

One day at recess time the son of our village's richest and most influential Turk came to school. He wanted us to have a wrestling match and selected me as a likely candidate. I refused because I knew Hodja did not approve, but he promised that he would not let Hodja punish me.

One after another, the pupils of my age wrestled with me. I floored them all on the dusty floor. I was not a strongly built child—on the contrary, I was skinny and small, but I knew a few tricks in wrestling and I was using them skillfully.

Before recess was over, Hodja walked in and saw the schoolroom filled with dust so thick that you would think a tornado had struck it. It did not take long for the Hodja to get me. I looked around for help from that rich son (as he had promised), but he was not there. He had sneaked out. I had been betrayed and deceived.

I had to suffer the penalty—first degree punishment. One of the Kalfas wrapped his arms around my shoulders and Hodja started hitting on my back with the hickory branch; but on the second blow, our protector, Hamdi Chavush's son, Selaheddin Kalfa, intervened, and I was saved.

I learned, in my first contact with the Turks, not to trust them. In the meantime, I was confused because another Turk had saved me from a terrible beating which perhaps would have no ending, at a time when the rest of the Kalfas were jealous of my wrestling ability and would not interfere to save a Mohammedan Armenian's hide.

Selaheddin was an exceptional Turk. He was as good-hearted and friendly as any Armenian boy. He stayed that way all his life. I wonder if he is still alive.

6

My Mother And Father

My mother could not read nor write, but it does not matter, because none of the women could. In their time, there were no schools for girls. Girls were not supposed to be educated, they were supposed to be wiser than the men folks.

Yet, in spite of this, my mother was one of the smartest women in the village. She was very keen and once in a while would advise my father who was not as keen as she. My father could not stand this, so he would use his powerful voice to win an argument, and then walk out of the house.

My mother was very religious too—as all women are—pious, God-fearing, and goodhearted. On Sunday mornings and evenings she never missed church services—rain or snow, hot or cold.

My father used to go to church with Mother, but after the massacres he would not go.

Every Sunday morning the same conversation took place between my father and my mother.

Mother would say, "Eh, Mart, (man) why don't you go someplace where people are praying to God? I don't care whether that place is a Protestant Church, old Armenian Church, or a mosque. Go and pray anywhere where people are gathered to pray. You don't like the minister, the priest, or the Hodja. What will happen to you when you die?"

"Don't worry about me when I am dead," Father would answer. "I will be responsible for my bad or good deeds. Keep this in your head woman. I will never sit in front of a Protestant minister. They are no good. They are not Christ's real servants. They do not believe in God. They are not sincere. If they were God's real servants, they would not deny Him and become Mohammedans. They would rather die or be massacred like Der Hovhannes, the other priest. He was a real genuine priest. He died like a martyr, Bible in hand, praying to God to forgive his torturers, like Jesus Christ did. They tortured him to deny his Christ. They suggested that if he became a Mohammedan, they would spare his life. No, he did not do it, he did not deny Him. He was a real priest—a real believer of what he was preaching. They tortured him, but all in vain. They could not make him alter his belief. They killed him. They poured kerosene on his body and burned him. I saw his charred body, in front of his vineyard's cave, where he had gone to hide himself, but they hounded and killed him. I saw the half-burned Bible lying nearby. He was a real priest, not a fake. Woman, bring him back to me and not only will I go to church but I will take my bed to church and sleep there day and night."

"Hey, Mart," my mother would argue again, "why are you blaming the minister or the priest? You yourself denied our Christ. We, all the village folks denied Him. Why blame them only?"

"Hey, woman," my father would argue again. "Your hair is long, but your brain is short. You do not understand these things. I am only a butcher, but they are servants of God. My life belongs to me. Their lives belong to God and Christ. I am making a living, an honest living, by killing and selling lamb. They are making their living by serving Christ.

They vowed their lives to Christ when they took the oath of their service. Yes, they should abide by that oath and die for Christ."

"Der Hovhannes baba was one in ten thousand," Mother would say. "It is wonderful to be a martyr like him, but I cannot blame the others who could not make the supreme sacrifice. They accepted Mohammedanism not with their hearts, but superficially, and the moment they had the chance, they again denied Mohammed as you and all the Community."

"You are chattering like a parrot," my father would say angrily. "Instead of using your brain, you would rather use your tongue. I don't want to listen to you. I don't want to step into any Protestant or Armenian Church and that is that."

And he would put the little flat bottle of gin in his coat pocket, walk out of the house, and go to the vineyard to water the vegetables or take care of the grapevines.

When the church services were over, and everyone left Church for their homes, my father would come back for his Sunday dinner.

7

The Dervish And My Uncle

It would not be a bad idea, perhaps, to get acquainted with some of my village folks so that you may better understand my countrymen. I will not bore you with lengthy descriptions of their mode of dress, habits of living, etc., but I am going to relate some of the little incidents which occurred, in an effort to acquaint you with these village folk.

The first will be my uncle, since I have told you some about my father and mother.

It was in April, the time when all the birds migrated back from the south and repaired their nests. The beggars of the country would follow them.

One day in the darkness, a dervish had sneaked in with the beggars. A dervish is the poorest of all beggars, something like a hermit or prophet, but lacking their education, wisdom, and vision. He would have a piece of clothing around his hips, a goatskin over his shoulder, long hair on his head, and a beard and mustache. He would be naked and barefooted. His body, being exposed to the sun throughout his lifetime, would be like bronze. He would carry in one hand a half coconut shell, hung from three fine chains; and in the other hand, a stick. The half coconut, or the Keshkur, as it was called, was used either to collect money in, as a cup to drink water from, or as a plate to eat food from. He would use the stick either to lean on when walking, or to chase dogs away when they tried to bite him.

He would stand in the market place and repeat the same sentence from sunrise to sundown, "ALLAH, GRANT ME THE PRICE OF A LOAF OF BREAD." He would not beg directly from men, but he would ask Allah to grant him a loaf of bread. Most of the time he would have enough patience to wait until Allah answered his plea, but sometimes, whenever he saw the opportunity, he would climb the minaret and ask a big ransom, threatening to commit suicide by jumping down from it. The Turks were aware of this, so at the very sight of one of these dervishes, they would rush to the mosque and lock the door of the minaret.

This dervish, however, was foxier than the Turks in the village. He had chosen the darkness of the night to enter the village and climb the minaret, and stayed there until the businessmen started opening their shops. Then he started his prayer—"ALLAH, SEND ME A MEJIDIYE (silver dollar) OR I'LL JUMP DOWN AND KILL MYSELF."

The villagers heard the voice and everybody, Armenian and Turk, gathered around the mosque. The dervish continued his prayer in a loud voice. The chances were very slim that the dervish would throw himself down, because life is so dear—but you cannot tell—sometimes in desperation a man does the least expected.

The dervish repeated his prayer and threat. He leaned out over the parapet of the minaret walkway and his body remained in that position. A shudder passed through the villagers. Suppose he lost his balance and fell head first to the pavement.

Then, by the laws of Islam, if human blood pours inside or outside of the mosque, that mosque becomes cursed and should be closed forever.

It was the responsibility of the Turks to raise that silver mejediah. There was considerable commotion and confusion among the Turks, but not one of them seemed ready to part with his nickel.

The dervish was repeating his prayer, his threat—"ALLAH, SEND ME ONE MEJIDIYE," and he leaned further over the parapet.

My Uncle Mikael sized up the situation. He knew well that the Turks would rather take the chance of closing their mosque than to part with a silver coin. He knew also that the dervish could, in desperation, or by accident, kill himself. In that case, the mosque would be closed, and they would confiscate the Armenian Church—the beautiful, magnificent, cut stone building towering over the village, and turn it into a mosque. That thought, that threat always present in the minds of Turks, forced my uncle to take charge of the situation.

He took a discarded, worthless copper coin, the size of a mejediah, to the tin-plating shop and had it plated.

Standing in the courtyard of the mosque holding this tin plated copper coin in his fingers, he pointed to the dervish and shouted with his powerful voice, "Dervish baba, here is your mejidiye. Get ready, I am coming up to bring it to you."

He walked towards the entrance of the minaret. The people held their breath. He entered it. He climbed the winding stairs. The dervish was waiting silently near the entrance. My uncle stood at the entrance and stretched the coin to the dervish. When the dervish tried to take it, my uncle grabbed him by the arm and pulled him inside the entrance and down the stairs to the courtyard.

The Turks patted my uncle's back. The dervish looked at the coin and noticed that it was worthless. He cried out loud like a child, then threw himself down to the pavement and rolled over and over again.

My Uncle Mikael became a hero. The Turks and Armenians for once were happy together, except the dervish who was squatting on the pavement and sobbing. He was hungry and he could not beg because everybody was angry with him. They chased him out of the village.

8

My Cousin "Arab"

"Arab" was a nickname. They called my cousin "Arab" because he had a very dark complexion.

In our part of the country we did not have Negroes; the only dark people with whom we came into contact were the nomadic Arabs, who sunburned while tending their flock of sheep or camels in the desert. They brought their sheep, and sometimes salt, loaded on their camels, to sell in our tiny marketplace. They were half naked, and almost as dark as a negro.

My cousin "Arab" was not as dark as they, but it was a nickname well suited to him, and it seemed that he was very proud of it. Nobody knew his real name. Maybe he himself had forgotten it. He was "Arab" even to his father and mother.

Arab's father, my uncle, was rich, intelligent and dignified. He would go into the lands of the Arabs and the Kurdish Tribes who were sheep and goat herders. He dressed just like an Arab sheik and rode his Arabian stallion, followed by his faithful Mohammedan shepherds. He carried all his gold in a belt tied to his waist. He carried no weapon because he did not need one. All the sheiks and all the tribe chieftains knew him and respected him. No thief, no highway robber dared to harm or rob him, because they knew he had the protection of the sheiks and tribe chieftains.

His son, Arab, was like his father, and even more so. He had followed the footsteps of his father. He took his father's business over when he died. He was very courageous—one of the very few Armenians in the village who was not afraid of the Turks.

One day a Turk had an argument with him in the marketplace of the village. As it was the habit of the Mohammedans, when they become angry with an Armenian, they insulted his Christian faith. This Turk was no exception, so he started calling my cousin "Kafir, Gavor, (infidel, unbeliever) Hachene, Putena, I will _ _ _ on your cross, on your church."

My cousin was not the one to keep quiet, so he shouted, "And I do the same thing on your mosque and on the candle in the mosque and on the oil in the candle, and on the wick in the oil."

The Turk could not stand this insult to his religion and to his objects of faith. He pulled out his gun from its holster. My cousin also pulled his gun out. Yes, he was the only Armenian in the village that carried a gun. The other Armenians did not dare to carry even a knife larger than six inches.

An army major, a Binbashi who was sitting on a chair in front of the café-house, jumped to his feet, held my cousin's arm and pulled him aside. He shouted to the Turk and all the others gathered around them who were seething with anger and ready to tear my cousin to pieces.

"I saw and heard all that happened here between Arab and that Turk. Arab insulted our religion, yes, but the Turk was the first one who incited him to do so. If our religion, our belief is sacred for us, the same is true for any Armenian's Christian faith. If we want that no one should insult our belief, none of us should insult their belief. I am glad that Arab, a brave, young man, had the courage and the audacity to answer back and did not keep quiet like most of his race was doing in a case like this. I hate cowards." He finished his speech and turned around and kissed my cousin Arab's forehead.

The mob dispersed slowly, but they were still angry. Well, there were not very many "Arabs" among Armenians, brave, audacious, and unafraid; and there were not very many Binbashis considerate enough to respect the other man's feelings, beliefs, thoughts, and human rights.

9

The Lie

Professor Tenekejian was my teacher at Euphrates College, an institution established by American missionaries in my hometown. He was a well educated man, a gentleman, and a scholar. As a matter of fact, he was considered the most educated man in the entire state. He was fatherly and dignified. We, the students, respected and loved him—we almost worshipped him.

One morning when we went to college, we were informed that during the night the Turkish government had put him in jail. He was a very kindly man, a good-hearted man, he would not hurt anybody. He would not even "step on an ant in order not to hurt it" as the saying goes. Why was he put then in prison? We soon learned that he was not the only Armenian that they had put in prison—thirty other men—teachers from other Armenian schools, merchants, artisans, etc. All the leaders of the Armenian communities of that big city were put in prison.

The Armenians were stunned, petrified, and were full of terror of another massacre. It was three months later when they started their trial, we learned about their accusation.

Two members of the Armenian Hunchag Revolutionary Party, Hapet and Hagop, who had come secretly from another part of the country into our town, had visited the accused and had talked to them.

They had come into the college and had talked to the professor. He did not belong to the party. He was not a revolutionist. He was not even a politician. He was a teacher who was minding his own business. It is not natural for everybody to be a fighter, a brave, a hero, or a revolutionist. There are very few who will risk their lives, their well-being, and their happiness for the sake of their nation, for the good of their people.

Hagop and Hapet belonged to the very few. They were trying to organize the Armenians for self-defense, to fight for their rights, for their honor, and for their lives. An impossible task, indeed, because what could a handful of Armenians do without arms and without organization? A minority in every part of the country among the Turks and Kurds who, by the permission of the government, were openly armed to their teeth. Their homes were full of arms and ammunition. They had the army, the guns, the cannons, and the bayonets; but for the Armenian it was forbidden to possess a gun, a revolver, or even a knife larger than six inches long.

Once in a while, Turkish gendarmes suddenly would enter an Armenian's house, turn everything upside down, look in every corner and closet, dig up the floors, tear down the walls and ceilings in search of concealed weapons. If they found anything that resembled a weapon, the father and older son of the house would be taken to jail and would be beaten, tortured, maimed, and kept there to rot, in order to serve as an example for the rest of the Armenians.

What could the Armenians do in a situation like this? For that matter, what could any man, European or American do?

Hagop and Hapet, two young men, were trying to do the impossible. They were trying to organize their fellow

Armenians, not to fight against the Turkish Army or the Turkish nation, far from it, but to be ready for self-defense, so that when the Turkish and Kurdish mobs attacked them, they, in turn, would be able to kill in self-defense. The Armenians under the tyrannical rule of the Turks had lost the sense of self-defense. They were downtrodden, oppressed, treated like slaves and worse than slaves, because slaves enjoyed the protection of their masters, while the Armenians did not even have that protection of their rulers. They were RAYAS. The government would not protect them against oppressors and torturers. The government itself was the oppressor, the torturer, and the murderer. The Islam population, the slum of the Turks, Kurds, Cherkezes, Lazes, etc., were the voluntary tools to carry out the massacres and the plundering.

Hagop and Hapet wanted to organize the Armenians and to make them aware of the dignity of themselves. But somebody had betrayed them and had informed the government. The secret police had followed their footsteps.

When a race is down and out, the "skunks" of that nation always get the field. They betray in the hope of receiving favors from their masters. The Turks were wise enough to take advantage of this situation. They would use these "skunks" to get all the secret information they could, but after their usefulness was over they would discard them so that their own countrymen would kill them in revenge. The Turks believed that any man who is low enough to betray his own race for personal gain would surely betray the ruling race when he gets the chance. They would stand the sight of these "skunks" as long as they could benefit from them, but as soon as their usefulness was over, their presence was intolerable, detestable, and hateful. "Once a traitor, always a traitor" was their logic.

Hagop and Hapet, being betrayed, were followed by the secret police, and whomever they contacted or talked with were under suspicion and were arrested. After three long months of agony in the dungeon, the trial started. It lasted a full month. At the end of the trial Professor Tenekejian and twenty-three others were found not guilty. Four were committed to life imprisonment. The verdict was sent to Sultan Abdul Hamid and it was sustained.

Hagop and Hapet were condemned to die. Three weeks later, one morning when the students were on their way to college and were passing through the marketplace, they had witnessed the decapitation of Hagop and Hapet. Their hands were tied behind their backs—they were made to kneel down—and the jellad (executioner) with his yataghan (heavy sabre) had chopped off their heads.

The entire student body was sad. It was terrible. We all hoped, up until the last minute that the French and American Consuls would intervene and get a change of verdict—life imprisonment.

When Professor Tenekejian heard the sad news, he could not control himself, and the tears flowed down his cheeks. It was stunning and petrifying. The bell rang and we all went to our classes. Professor Tenekejian was very sad. He was lecturing on the French Revolution, and he had told us not to take any notes—no pencils, no paper. This kind of teaching was forbidden. Not only that, but even the words "revolution," "freedom," "Armenian," "nation," and "justice," were taboo. Anyone who dared to speak or write these words in a book or in a copy book was condemned to the dungeon.

The professor wanted to lecture about Bastille Day, July 14th. He did not know how to start, when all of the sudden, out of a clear sky one of the classmates, who had been present at the trial asked him, "Professor, at the trial when the judge asked you, "Have you ever met these revolutionaries?" you answered "No, your Honor, I haven't met them." I saw with my own eyes that you and they met at our campus gate. Was not that a lie? Why did you not tell the truth?"

As if the torture that our poor professor had just undergone was not enough, this foolish student had to ask a question such as this. The poor professor's pale face turned red. There was anger in his eye, but he controlled himself and kept quiet for a minute—then he began—"I think it is more important that on a day like this, instead of talking about the French Revolution, we talk about the revolution of our thoughts and of our way of thinking.

"This institution is founded by American missionaries whose prime purpose is to teach us the Bible and the moral principles contained in the Bible. One of these principles is DO NOT LIE. Our missionaries are putting a big accent on it. They are pounding it into our skulls, day in and day out, "DO NOT LIE." But what is a lie? That is the question. There are all kinds of lies; big lies and little lies, harmless lies and harmful lies; useful white lies and dangerous black lies. For example: The lie of Santa Claus is a harmless lie. What fool would rob a child of his or her happy imagination by telling him or her that there is no Santa Claus? Who would dare to tell to a sick mother who is in bed, the truth about her son who is dead in a far away country? That too is a useful lie.

"DO NOT LIE, yes, that is the order of God, but that same God has given you your brain, your power of thought and judgment so that you will think and judge for yourself.

"DO NOT LIE, yes if that lie is intended to cheat others for your own selfish interest. In that case, honesty is the best policy. You should not cheat, you should not lie, you should tell the truth, the whole truth, and nothing but the truth. But if telling the truth is going to give our torturer, the Turk, a chance or an alibi to put the victim in jail, to torture him and decapitate him, then telling the truth is Asinine, with a capital "A," pure and simple.

"I lied, yes. And I would lie again and again to save my life or any Armenian's life. I would rather die and go to hell, than let anyone of my Armenians suffer at the hands of these cruel barbarians, by telling them the truth.

"The Turks, our oppressors, are ganged up against us. We cannot betray our own nationalities by telling them the truth. Telling the truth, in a case like this, is not Christianity. It is stupidity and asininity.

"I lied, and I am not sorry, but I am sorry that my lie could not save those two young and patriotic Armenians who are decapitated today."

He could not continue any more. The tears fell from his eyes and rolled down his cheeks and were lost in his beard.

We all cried except that stupid jackass of a student who was too confused in his mind about the white and black lies.

10

Liberty, Equality, And Fraternity

1908—July 10th

This is the day that the despotic government of Sultan Abdul Hamid was thrown out by the young Turks and a constitutional government was formed. It was patterned after the Republic of France.

"Liberty," "Fraternity," and "Equality" were the mottos. We were all free; brothers, and equal in the eyes of the law. No more ruling nation, no more ruled races. We were all Osmanlis. The country belonged to everybody. Turk, Armenian, Kurd, Greek, Cherkez, and Jew were all alike—equal.

No more oppressor; no more oppressed.

The government in Constantinople was in the hands of the young Turks, educated mostly in France or in Germany. After this, we were going to be treated like human beings. Armenian Revolutionary Leaders in Constantinople were being embraced by these young Turks. Our political prisoners were liberated, and they were treated as heroes. The younger generation of Armenians was happy—deliriously happy. The older generation of Armenians were suspicious, and the Turks were silent.

For six hundred years they, the Turks and Armenians, had lived as masters and servants, or as lords and pariahs, and suddenly, in twenty-four hours, they were declared equals. For six hundred years they had lived side by side as Mohammedans and Christians. The Mohammedans had despised and looked down on the Christians. They had called them Kafir (infidel) and hated them for their faith. Now, suddenly, in twenty-four hours, they were brothers.

The Christians could not believe it. The Mohammedans could not believe it either, but the crowd, the mob was shouting, "Long Live Equality, Liberty, and Fraternity." The banners were waving, the leaders were preaching, the paraders were marching, the exiles were returning, the prisons were being emptied, and we could travel wherever we wished without a permit—an unbelievable fact.

Soon, the people's deputies were chosen, and the Parliament was opened. We even had our own representatives—eight Armenian deputies, brilliant speakers all of them, well honored and well received. We were really and truly "equals—brothers—free!"

Only nine months later, in the month of April, 1909, on Palm Sunday, the Armenians in Cilicia, along the shores of the Mediterranean Sea, were massacred. Cilicia was the only part of the country that Sultan Abdul Hamid had spared in 1895, and they were not massacred, but now, the young Turks were finishing Abdul Hamid's sinister job, some thirteen years later.

Thirty thousand Armenians were massacred. Yes, old Turk and young Turk—they are all alike—always a Turk. Democratic Turk, or despotic Turk, a Turk with a fez and Shalvar, or a Turk with a hat and trousers—it does not make any difference. A Turk is a Tartar in heart and blood. You can change the outward appearance of a Turk, you can educate him and he will act scholarly, gentlemanly, but scratch his skin and you will find the Tartar—ferocious and bloodthirsty.

Thirty thousand Armenians were massacred, their homes plundered, robbed, burned down, and thousands of orphans and widows were left to make their way in life.

The crime was committed with the full knowledge of the Central Government in Constantinople, because in Turkey, nothing could take place without its full approval.

The civilized world soon heard about it and the young Turks lost their prestige. They ran for cover.

The government sent a delegation headed by an Armenian, Babigian, a member of Parliament, to investigate and determine those responsible. He spent some time in Cilicia, then he returned to Constantinople and started preparing his documentary report. The night before the day that he was to present his report in Parliament, he was found dead in his bed.

The Armenians whispered, "They killed Babigian."

The Turks said, "Babigian died of a heart attack."

His report was lost. No one knew what had happened to his report. It had vanished, with his death.

The days, weeks, and months passed by. The ambassadors were silent and the civilized world soon forgot. "Equality," "Fraternity," and "Liberty" were dead.

Hamid was deposed, but his spirit was ruling through thousands of other "Hamids" under the name of young Turks.

A Turk is a Turk, and a Turk will always remain a Turk.

Graduation from Euphrates College in 1910. Garabed is in the second row, fourth from right.

11

Ali Effendi, The Ulema

Ali Effendi, the Ulema (scholar of the Koran) was a tall and husky man, and although always well dressed and clean, you could not see his dress, because he always wore a jubbah (tunic) over his clothes—as it is the custom for all Moslem ulemas.

His face had a dignified appearance, covered with a mustache and beard. Around his red fez was wrapped a clean, white turban that was thicker than his arms. His ancestors were princes, and his behavior was that of one who was proud of his heritage.

In spite of his princely background and his great wealth from his farms, he was well educated. This is unusual, because in Turkey, they believe that the princes shall not work or study. Work is for the common people, while leisure is for the princes. They rode horses and went hunting with their servants and hunting dogs, or they went to their farms to collect their share of farm produce. When out for a stroll they walked very slowly, slower than a tortoise, because that was considered a sign of dignity and nobility. Only servants or common people, or laborers walked fast or ran, but the princes literally crawled.

Our village folks would rise before sunrise and started walking fast on the highway to go to a nearby city (three miles away) to work. In the evening, just after sundown, they hurried back to the village. They walked as fast as they could, but lo; one of the princes would be walking on the highway very, very slowly. The Armenians would approach him and slow down. They would almost stand still, as no one dared to pass a prince—it was not considered proper, respectful; it was considered insolent and insulting to the dignity of a prince. Others would reach and join the previous arrivers, and finally a big crowd would form behind the prince, anxious to reach their homes. It was like a river suddenly stopped by a dam, forming a lake. This human river of Armenians, workers and laborers, would form a lake behind this human dam, the prince. The prince, aware of this, felt important and dignified, and his vanity being satisfied, once in a while, would pull himself aside on the highway and order magnanimously, "pass my sons." The lake would form a river and in passing him, they would bow down in reverence. They would salute him by raising their right hands to their mouths and then to their foreheads.

In a democratic country like America, it is difficult to understand and visualize the life that was ours. In spite of all that, we were still contented and praising God that we were alive, perhaps because we did not know any better or were helpless, or perhaps both.

But Ali Effendi was altogether different from all of the other princes. He was a student and a scholar of the Koran and the Bible. Yes, the Bible. Very surprising, indeed, for an Islam ulema. He was broad-minded and tolerant towards the Christians. For this reason, he allowed me to sit down beside him, although I, an Armenian and Christian, was despised by other Turks and Moslems. No, Ali Effendi was not like them.

We talked about the Koran and about the Bible. He recognized Moses as a prophet of God. He thought about Haziret Issa (Christ) as a prophet. He had respect for both of them. He would not mention their names without adding the word, Haziret (Saint). They were both saints and prophets to him.

"Moses, no doubt, was a great prophet in his time," he would tell me. "Centuries later, came Christ who was certainly familiar with the Mosaic law and he added his own to it. Therefore, he was a greater prophet than Moses. Mohammed, the latest of them all, was the greatest, because he was familiar with both the Mosaic and the Christian religions, and he added his own to them." "Another thing," he would say, "do you know something that is written in the New Testament? 'And he said unto his disciples, Go ye and preach the Gospel to the four corners of the earth.' This means conclusively that Christ had a written Gospel in his hand to which he was referring. Now that Gospel is lost. You do not have it. What you have in your hand is what his disciples have written. The present Gospel is not Christ's original Gospel."

I had never thought of that myself, I admitted. Therefore, the next day I asked Reverend Carey, our Bible teacher, about it. "The word 'Gospel' means tidings, glad news, not a written book," he explained.

I conveyed that answer to Ali Effendi.

"It is as plain as the nose on my face," he objected. "In my Injil Sheriff (New Testament) it says plainly Ingil (Gospel) not Havadis (Tidings)."

Ali Effendi was just one among a thousand Turks. He belonged, as I mentioned before, to the ruling nation of Turkey. He belonged to nobility. His parents were pashas. He was an ulema (a wise man), but he was friendly to me. He was an exceptional Turk. He liked me and I liked him. Therefore, when I had to leave my home to go to Constantinople to study engineering and I visited my friends and relations to bid them good-bye. I also visited Ali Effendi in his mansion. He was in his Selamlik (male visitors quarters) squatted on a divan, a rosary in his hand, meditating.

"Selamen Aleykum, Ali Effendi," I saluted him.

"Aleykum Selam," (welcome to my home) he answered.

"I am going to Constantinople to study. I came to bid you good-bye," I said.

"God be with you and grant you success," and he added, "But, by-the-way, do you have enough money to finance your education? I know that your father is poor and can scarcely take care of his family's bare necessities."

"I have just enough money, Ali Effendi, to pay for my journey and to live a month in Constantinople. In the meantime, I am going to try to win a scholarship from the government. Besides, I shall write to my brothers in the U.S.A. for assistance, if they can afford it."

"Write to your brothers, and try to win the scholarship," said Ali Effendi. "In case your brothers cannot help, or you do not win the scholarship, remember me. I am ready and willing to finance you, to help you until you finish your education. I like you and I will pray for your success. This country needs educated men like you." I thanked him for his kind thoughts and good heart, kissed his hand, said good-bye and departed.

Three weeks later I arrived in Constantinople. I rented a barren room in a han (inn), spread my carpet over the earthen floor and placed my mattress over it. I squatted on it, and wrote a letter to my brothers about my venture and asked for their help. Then I began to study for the entrance examinations.

It was three weeks later when I received a letter from Ali Effendi. He wrote, "You arrived in Constantinople but you didn't write to me. I got your address from your younger brother, Aharon, and I am writing to you. When you said good-bye to me I promised you all the financial aid you may need for your education. Maybe you thought it was an act of politeness. By this letter, I want you to know that I meant every word of my promise. Don't worry, I am ready and willing to help you until you finish your education."

I thanked him for his kindness and generosity, because I had already won the scholarship, and I did not need his help, but I did not forget and never will forget his kindness.

Yes indeed, there were good Turks, but very, very few.

The engineering college that I was admitted to was a government supported boarding school. In that year thirty new students were to be admitted by written tests. Three hundred participated in these tests, and only thirty were selected. Out of that thirty, three were non-Mohammedans, one was a Jew, one a Greek, and one an Armenian. They were admitted to prove to the outside world that in Turkey there was "Liberty," "Equality," "Fraternity," and above all "Justice."

I was the lucky Armenian.

Another Armenian had been accepted the same way the previous year. Therefore, we were two Armenians, one Greek, one Jew, among one hundred forty-six Mohammedan students.

All the teachers were Mohammedans, and I will confess, that both teachers and students were very, very friendly to us.

Everything was "fine and dandy," smooth and peaceful. until the day when the Balkan War was declared.

Bulgars, Greeks and Serbians united and attacked Turkey. It was a surprise attack. The Turks were not prepared and their army was defeated very badly on every front and retreating, fortified cities were falling one after the other.

12

The Balkan War And The Volunteers

There was a meeting in our school. The students were called together to see what they could do in order to help their country in this hour of defeat, misery and despair. As soon as the meeting was opened, all the rabble-rousers, one after the other, got up on the pulpit and started pouring out all the clichés of brilliant words they had memorized about their fatherland, about the noble and brave Turks, about Islam pure and true, about their flag, their ancestors, and their glorious past.

They were pouring forth hateful words against the Kafir's, the Christian pigs, the infidel dogs, the barbars, and the massacrers. They were trying to arouse the fanaticism, the chauvinism dormant in their fellow students. And were they successful!

Huddled in the far end corner of the hall with the other Armenian student, we watched their frenzy, their anger and their blood pressure going higher, higher and higher, ready to burst. Their eyes were red, their faces were pale, and their fists were clinched. They were not students anymore, they were not human, they were a frenzied-mob. They were beasts, ferocious beasts; ready to kill, to murder, to cut anything or anybody to pieces, that was related to Christianity.

We Armenians huddled in that corner, were pale, shivering, shuddering, helpless, and most of all expecting any minute to be attacked, to be knocked down, trampled, and killed. We were expecting to be the first victims of the insults that the "Christian Barbarians" were piling every minute on their glorious nation, on their most sacred religion.

The frenzied, the raged eyes were turning back and staring at us. We could hear their teeth gnashing.

All of a sudden, one of the most ardent fanatic mobsman of them all, asked for volunteers. Volunteers who would go to the front to extol the soldiers, in order to stay and fight, and stop the invading "Christian dogs," in their forward march, chase them back and save their beloved fatherland — Turkey, and their pure faith — Islamism. Yes, volunteers, volunteers, they seconded from everywhere.

The motion was carried, and the hall was silent, silent like a cemetery. One could hear the ghosts whispering. "Who wants to be a volunteer?" one of the rabble-rousers asked. All the eyes were turned toward the ones that were hollering the loudest, the ones that were eager to show their high degree of patriotism, the ones that were claiming that in their veins was running the pure blood of their ancestors, heroic and brave.

They volunteered. They had to volunteer. After all those fiery eloquent speeches, they had to, there was no way out of it. Seven volunteers, all in all. The others were silent. Their lips were clamped. Who would be foolish enough to leave the comfortable bed, the delicious cooking, and discontinue the education?

It was all right to be patriotic and let the others fight and get killed for the glory of the mother country, for the faith of Islam. Let the others be the heroes of the Vatan (country), the Shehids (martyr) for the faith. They would applaud, they would parade, they would wave flags, they would pat the other's back, they would eulogize, but they themselves would keep away from that heroism, from that martyrdom.

They wanted to stay alive. They did not want to be killed. Seven volunteers and no more.

The balloon had burst. They all had cooled down, humility had settled in, their fury gone. The fire in their eyes was out, the pale of their face vanished. Their teeth were not gnashing anymore, their fists were loose, their hands were limp, and the lions of the minute ago were turned into sheep with the foolish, sheepish dim light in their eyes.

We were forgotten, the two Armenians. They were busy now with their humility and shame, with their deflated egos.

Deep in their hearts they knew they were deserters. They were traitors, but life was too dear to be endangered. They were debating in their own minds. The struggle inside their brains was between patriotism and selfishness, between fanaticism and cold reasoning.

It is hard, very hard to die, even for your own country, even for your own faith. They were educated people, students, effendis; future engineers. The country would need them to build road, bridges, railroads, and waterways. They were important for the future development of the country. The government needed them for the future, yes, that was the reason they were exempted from military service. The government had not drafted them, why should they volunteer?

At the end the selfishness, the cold reasoning had conquered. And we, two Armenians, were glad.

No more volunteers; only seven of them.

Early in the morning the seven packed their clothing in a bag, shouldered them, and marched out of school. They went, knowing in their own hearts they were the "damn fools" that were caught in their own traps. They were not patriots, but show offs, and they were going because there was no way out of it. They went, and the rest of the student body, in their own hearts, were thinking, "the damn fools."

The war was continuing, the Turkish army was retreating, Salonika surrendered. Yanina and Adrianapolis were still holding, although surrounded. The Turks were fortifying Chatalja, the last line of defense. The streets of Constantinople, public places, mosque yards, and schools were crowded with Mohammedan emigrants who had escaped before the invading armies.

Poverty, filth, hunger, cold and dysentery were raising havoc amongst them. Death was everywhere. People were dying on the sidewalks. One could clearly hear the booming of the cannons. Bulgars were knocking at the gates of Constantinople. They were trying to capture it, to liberate it, liberate the Church of Saint Sophia, the symbol of Christianity, and erect the Golden Cross on top of its dome.

Those were gloomy days for the Turks. They were being chased off European soil.

Scarcely a week had gone by since that meeting, when one morning our seven volunteers walked in through the gate of the Engineering Building, bundles on their backs, unshaven, tired, filthy, and lousy. They were disgusted, their egos had deflated. They were weak and humbled. They were very eager to talk, in order to justify their return; their inglorious retreat. They still claimed to be patriotic, ready to sacrifice their lives for their dear old glorious Ottoman Empire, to protect its boundaries against the invaders, but alas, they had been unable to find any officer of the army that would appreciate their willingness, their readiness, and their patriotism. They were sent from one officer to another, from one army camp to another. It seems the officers had enough trouble with their own regular soldiers to burden themselves with volunteers.

It seems that what they needed wasn't "sissified intellectuals," but hardboiled soldiers who would dig in and fight, would kill and stop the enemy in its tracks. Who wanted to be bothered with seven students, hotheaded, uncontrollable, wise and educated asses?

Nobody, they had to return! That was their story.

The Turks, at the last minute, driven to desperation, succeeded in organizing their demoralized army which stood at Chatalja. With their machine guns nested on the slope, they mowed down the attacking Bulgars in the plain and stopped them at the gates of Constantinople. The rest is history, a sad and tragic history of the conquerors when they tried to divide the spoils.

The Serbs and the Greeks together attacked their allies, the Bulgars, who had suffered the most and who carried the ball to the goal. They attacked their ally and took away from him what he had gained from the Turks with the blood of its youth.

The Turks took advantage of this treachery and attacked and regained part of their lost territory—Thrace.

They weren't kicked out of Europe, they are still there.

No wonder, right at this instant, the Bulgars hated the Greeks and the Serbians worse than they did the Turks. Why? Because the Turks were their enemies, but the Greeks and the Serbs were supposed to be their friends. They were the valiant fighters and in the victory they were stabbed behind their backs by their friends.

They couldn't forget it, and they hated them. They still can't forget it and they still hate them.

13

Against My Will, I Became A Leader

The Balkan War was over. Those wounded soldiers who survived were transferred to other places. Our school resumed its normalcy. However, it was too good to be true.

On our school faculty there were two Belgian professors. They were lecturing in French and it was translated into Turkish for the benefit of those students who could not understand French. One of the translators was Tartar Mustafa, who, instead of translating the lecture as he should, always added his own comments. The students did not like this, so they asked the dean of the school to remove him. This, however, was not an easy matter because Tartar Mustafa was an "Ittihad." That is, a party member of high standing.

One morning, when Tartar Mustafa walked into the classroom and sat down on his chair, the entire classroom walked out on him. The dean ordered them back. They did not obey and were expelled from the school. The other students, in sympathy left their classrooms. The school was in turmoil. Classes were suspended. Hot heads, busybodies, rabble-rousers were on their jobs. Meetings, speeches, disturbances, but nothing constructive.

At noon time, a few of the rabble-rousers approached me and said, "we have a protest paper prepared, and every student has signed; but when we approached your fellow Armenians to sign, they looked for your signature, and not finding it they refused to sign."

"Let me have a look at your protest paper," I asked. I looked at it—just one line—'We the undersigned, protest the expulsion of the fourth class.' That was all, more or less.

"Do you think I would sign a paper like this?" I objected.

"What is wrong with it?" they asked me.

"The whole thing. First of all, you cannot protest against a decision if it is well-founded, reasonable, or justified. You can protest if the decision is unjust and unreasonable, and that should always be based on and proven by reasonable arguments and facts."

"What do you suggest then?" they asked me.

"First of all, in my opinion, the revolting class is guilty in its act, and the dean had every right to punish them. There is no justification for their act, but in our school by-laws, written and signed by the Director of Public Works Administration, no boarding student can be expelled from the school building. Mind you, he can be expelled from classes, yes, but not from the building. Nobody can throw him out on the street with no means of shelter and food. That is inhuman, that is cruel and that is exactly what the administration has done. Now our protest shall be based on their own by-laws."

"All right," they agreed, "let us have another meeting and explain your viewpoint. In five minutes all the students were gathered in the hall and I was in the pulpit addressing them. It did not take me five minutes, with my broken Turkish, to explain to the students my viewpoint. Scarcely had I finished my speech, when the hall thundered with hurrahs and applauding.

"Put it in writing! Put it in writing!" I could hear their shouts. "My Turkish is very poor, you all know that," I objected. "Let one of you better versed in your own language, write it down." "Nobody else but you must write it. We will correct your grammar," they shouted again. I sat down and wrote it. Scarcely had I finished it, when the students lined up to sign it. Half an hour later the protest was on its way to the Public Works Administration.

The following day two engineers from the Public Works Administration were in our school. They called me in, questioned me about the protest paper, put the questioning in writing, and asked me to sign it. I signed it. They went away and I reported it to the student body. Two days later, the Public Works Administrator himself came to the school. I was called in again. The Administrator, Burhan Bey, a tall athletic six-footer, rather good looking, with graying hair, was sitting at the table. Our assistant dean was sitting next to him—pale, shrunk, evidently alarmed. Our dean had already been fired as incompetent.

Burhan Bey started the questioning while I remained standing.

"What is your name?"

"Garabed."

"Where from?"

"Harput."

"How far is Harput from here?"

"Seventeen days journey in a covered wagon."

"You mean to tell me that from a distance of seventeen days journey you came here to disturb the peace and quiet of this school?"

"I refuse that statement, your honor."

"You refuse that statement? Who wrote that protest?" He shot the question.

"The day before yesterday I answered all those questions and signed a statement."

"If it becomes necessary to answer those questions a thousand times you must do it, you insolent, you ___ you ___." He was furious, but he still kept his temper.

"Now go ahead and tell me who wrote that protest!"

"They who signed it—the entire student body."

"Don't be so naïve. Who put that protest into writing? Whose penmanship is it? Answer me that."

"Mine," I answered.

"That means that you are the instigator, the agitator of this turmoil. You are the leader of this revolt."

"I refuse the accusation, your honor. I wish I had that superior mind that you are ascribing me. I wish I had the brain to be the leader of a student body of which most of them are in higher classes. It is an honor you bestow on me, your honor, but I am sorry. Everyone who signed that protest has as much judgment as I, and perhaps more than I."

"You are going too far with your demagoguery." He jumped to his feet. He was getting angrier with every question. He walked toward me and, I thought surely, he was going to slap me. I was becoming more and more afraid.

"Do you know that I have the authority to expel you from this school?"

"Certainly I do," I answered, and I knew that I was pale. My knees were sagging, and I could feel a cold sweat covering my whole body. To be expelled from school—the thought was terrible.

During the turmoil, aside from the rebellious class, the Board of Student Association and several other students were expelled for minor offenses. Everybody, student, teacher, and administrator had become nervous, touchy, excitable, as they were expelling the students right and left.

"Get out of my sight before I lose my temper, you insolent imp!" he shouted. The Administrator looked like a giant to me, and the Assistant Dean had shrunk and was almost lost in his chair. I knew it was my turn to be expelled. I staggered out of the room. Students were waiting in the assembly hall. They were eager to hear my report. I reported all and added, "I think he is going to expel me." "Nobody can expel you!" shouted the students all together. "If they expel you, we shall all leave and get out of this building." They resolved and everybody signed the resolution.

The school monitors, always around the hallway, were reporting every movement of the student body to the Administration. They reported this decision too. They did not expel me.

The days were passing. The students were stubborn, and the Administration was even more so. We took our case to the newspapers, published in Turkish, Armenian, and Greek. We took our case to the Parliament. The entire country had heard about it. People would come and try to interfere, but they were all for the Administration. No one was for the students. Many days passed by. One morning, when a few of us boarders, who were in the school building, had gathered around the coal stove, sad and disgusted, a student walked in and with a note of anxiety said, "There are two engineers who are here to mediate, and some of our busybodies are over there talking to them and goofing up everything. Please hurry over."

"I am sick and tired of all this affair," I answered. "It was foolish from the start, and it is foolish now. I can't see any way out of it. I don't want to talk to anybody. We do not have any friends any more. All those that come here to talk are pro-Administration."

Those around me did not pay any attention to my bellyaching. They carried me forcibly into the room where two engineers were seated. Six of our busybodies were standing in front of them and talking.

Once in the room, the two engineers started questioning me, but they could not get any satisfactory answers from me. My answers were all cynical, scornful, with the result of hate and suspicion.

After five minutes of questioning one of them became angry.

"Enough of you, effendi," he shouted at me, "enough of those nasty answers. Listen here, we are engineers on the Samsun and Sivas Railroad. We read all about our school, our hearts bled, and we left our work, took the boat and crossed the Black sea to come here to see what we could do for our Alma Mater."

"Listen, effendi, we also are graduates of this school. Once, this was our nest as it is now yours. They are ruining that nest, and you, with your ignorance, stubbornness, foolishness, you are helping them to accomplish it."

The tears dropped from his eyes and his voice quivered, but he continued. "We are your friends, believe us and trust us." In seeing the tears rolling down his cheeks, I realized how foolish I had been.

"I am ready," I volunteered. "Ask and you will be answered."

"All right. Now, what are you asking?"

"Tartar Mustafa, the cause of all this, must be fired."

"He has resigned already."

"The fourth class and all the others who were expelled for any reason at all must be readmitted."

"They will be readmitted with no exception."

"Our dean must be reinstated."

"I am sorry. That cannot be done."

"Therefore..."

"Wait a minute. Before we came here, we met your dean and he asked us to tell you not to insist on his return. He has already secured a position with an Electrical Company. He begs not to insist on his return."

"I believe in you."

"Have faith in our good intentions and we will see that you get all you want. God be with you." They stood up.

"God be with you."

They shook hands with us and departed. Yes, the next day, every student was back in his class. Tartar Mustafa was out, so was the dean of our school.

One gain, one loss, and a whole month's schooling wasted. This was the result of that foolishness which made me, an Armenian, the leader of the entire Turkish student body.

14

Burhan Bey, The Gentleman

Our surveying class was in Keghad-Haneh.

We had pitched tents and were ready to survey the hills and valleys. There were twenty-eight students, divided into four groups.

I was the leader of one of the groups. It was our bad luck that our transit was a dilapidated, broken-down thing. We surely needed a new one, but the only place we could get one was the Public Works Administration.

I asked the boys of our group to go and get one, but no one would go. "You are the leader, you should provide one," was the answer. I pleaded, "you know that the Public Works Administrator is Burhan Bey. You also know how much he hates me. He still considers me responsible for all the turmoil in the school and for all the humiliation to which he was subjected. Surely this will give him a chance to get even with me, 'the insolent imp.'" "We don't care, that is your problem. You are our leader. It is your responsibility," was their foolish and stubborn reply.

It is not that they wanted to be mean to me, or that they were jealous of me, an Armenian being their leader, no, far from it. They were all bashful, backward, full of oriental inferiority complex, which made it hard for them to come in contact with high government officials.

There was nothing left for me to do but take the boat of Golden Horn and face the men who had threatened to expel me from school. When the boat docked at the Galata Bridge I got out and started climbing the Bab-Ali Avenue where the Public Works Ministry Building was located. I climbed the steps, stood at the door of the Public Works Administrator, took a deep breath, and rang the doorbell. My heart was beating heavily.

"Come in," said a voice.

I opened the door. Burhan Bey was seated at his desk, facing the door. He looked at me, recognized me, and jumped to his feet with open arms.

"Hayir ola, (may it be good) Garabed effendi. Which wind blew you into this office?" He walked toward me and with both hands grasped my hands. I was surprised, overwhelmed.

"Hayir dir (it is good), Burhan Bey," I saluted him quickly and explained the purpose of my visit.

"Take a seat. Make yourself comfortable. Have a cup of coffee."

"Thank you, Burhan Bey. I don't have much time to spare. The group is waiting for me," I apologized.

He rang the bell. A minute later the custodian of the equipment knocked on the door and entered.

"Hassan, take Garabed effendi into the warehouse and let him choose the best transit that can be found in the place. Let him take it with him." and he added, "Listen, Hassan, do not ask any receipt from him! Trust him, I do trust him."

I thanked him a thousand times, and followed Hassan into the warehouse where I picked a brand new transit.

On my way back in the boat, my thoughts were about the man who, four weeks ago, walked toward me in anger ready to slap me, but did not—who threatened to expel me from school, and did not. Now he greeted me with open arms, ready and willing to do anything for me. So gracious, so kind.

Why? Why was the devil of four weeks ago an angel today?

Your guess is just as good as mine.

Garabed, 29 years old, drafted as Turkish Engineer-Officer.

15

The Beginning Of The Tempest

1914, October

On every street corner in Constantinople they had glued a proclamation:

"I DECLARE MOBILIZATION AND CALL EVERY ABLE-BODIED MAN BETWEEN 18 AND 45, TO BEAR ARMS."

Signed-Minister of War,
Enver

I was able-bodied, between 18 and 45, and I was drafted. In this war, college students were not exempt as they were during the Balkan War.

After six months training, I was sent as an engineer to the Amanos Mountains, in Cilicia, to help build the highway that had to pass over the mountain range.

The famous Berlin-Baghdad Bahn (railroad) from either side had reached to the mountain range and stopped. The tunnel, five kilometers long, which would connect them, was not yet finished. It would take two more years to complete it. The highway, therefore, crossing over the hump of the mountain, had to connect both ends of the railroad.

I remember the exact date that I left Constantinople— February 21st, 1915.

I was happy, very happy that I did not have to go to the front. On my way to my destination, the train had to stop for two hours at the town of Tarsus. I took advantage of it and visited the Campus of Saint Paul's American College. I met some of the students there, all Armenians, and they informed me that the Armenian soldiers in the Turkish Army were being disarmed and sent into the Labor Battalions. This was to be the beginning of a tragedy unheard of in mankind's history.

I arrived at my destination, Kanli-Getchit (bloody pass), at the southern foot of the Amanos Mountains, where two tributaries of the Jeyhan River merged.

They gave me a tent, an orderly, and a horse. On February 25th I started to work on the road. They were widening and repairing the old existing road.

March 5th I saw fifteen Armenians from Zeytun, chained together by their arms and by their necks, surrounded by as many armed and mounted Turkish gendarmes. They were taking them to Osmaniye. The Turks working on the road were talking out loud and I could hear them.

"The traitors, the enemies of the fatherland, the revolutionaries of Zeytun. They revolted against the government, and the government has captured them and is going to hand them the the punishment they surely deserve."

Even under the burdens of their chains they had all the appearances of the heroic mountaineers, which they were for centuries.

March 20th, during the night, there was a big commotion around my tent. I woke up and listened. They had taken all the able-bodied Armenians from Dortyol and brought them here to work in Labor Battalions.

May 1st, at noontime, on the banks of the river, surrounded by gendarmes, a group of Armenians were herded together.

They were the first ones to be deported. Being an officer of the Turkish Army, I walked past the gendarmes and entered their camp. They were from Zeytun. Babo Agha, their leader, was squatted on the ground and the teacher of the same town was nearby.

"Parev (hello)," I said in Armenian.

"Parev," they answered suspiciously, obviously thinking I was a spy. I sat down. He was eating raisins produced in their own vineyards, which are famous for their taste and size in all Turkey. He handed me a handful of them. I did not want to take any. How could I take anything from them? Their destination and destiny unknown, they needed every bit of it.

"If you are a friend of us, take it or else I will consider you as an enemy," said Babo-agha. I had to take them and put them in my pocket.

"Babo-agha," I asked him after I had won his confidence, "the Turks around here are claiming that you Zeytun people revolted against the government and the government took punitive measures against you.

Babo-agha sighed and said, "I wish we had revolted and fought like our ancestors had done for centuries, died on our own soil and had not been subjugated to this disgrace—this disgrace of being herded together and carried away like sheep by these few lousy gendarmes. No, my son, this time we thought we should be loyal. We were advised by our higher religious authorities to stay loyal, be obedient to the government and not create any disturbances in its hour of trouble. We obeyed. We did not make any trouble and here we are. We should have fought and died there on the rocks where our forefathers died, but now it is too late."

He sighed and said no more.

The gendarmes ordered everybody to get up. I shook hands with Babo-agha and the teacher and we parted. They started their walk on the dusty road, men, young and old, women, young and old, and children. Walk, walk. Where to? Nobody knew.

Destination unknown, destiny known.

That same night, I sat down in my tent and wrote a long letter, rather a report to the editor of the Armenian Daily, "Azatamart," published in Constantinople. The editor, R. Zartarian, was my countryman. I knew him personally. He had been like a teacher and a father to me. After reporting this affair, I asked him to notify Zohrab and Vartkes, the most influential Armenian Representatives in the Parliament, to do their utmost to return these poor Armenians to their homeland, else all would die on the road from misery, filth, thirst, and hunger.

Years later I learned that while I was writing my letter in my tent, Zartarian, Vartkes, Zohrab, and three hundred other Armenian intellectuals were dragged out of their beds during the night and put in prison in order to be exiled, tortured, and killed by crushing their heads and pouring out their brains.

May 2nd, they charged me and my assistant Sebuh, another Armenian engineer, to survey the road from one end to the other, 110 kilometers long. We took the transit, rods, tents and six soldiers from the labor battalions and started to work.

16

The Hollow Pit

One week later we were in Hasanbeyli, an Armenian village hidden amongst the orchards. We visited the unfinished church on top of the hill, built in snow white cut stone. Nearby, in the limestone rock, there was a big hollow pit. We were shocked and stunned at the sight of so many skulls with so many cavities, which once were eyes, staring at us. Skeletons, arm bones, leg bones, vertebrae bones, large and small—full up to the brim of that huge pit.

These were the victims of the 1909 Palm Sunday massacres, killed by the young Turks, the civilized young Turks, just nine months after they had dethroned Sultan Abdul Hamid, "the damned," and declared constitutional government.

"Equality," "Fraternity," "Liberty," and "Justice."

The victims of that crime of which I had heard when I was still in my birthplace, were there in a pile in that pit. They were killed mercilessly, and those who were not killed, had gathered their skeletons in this pit as a monument for the barbarism of the Turk.

We left the place, tears in our eyes.

17

Great Is The Power Of Christ

Next day was a sad day. Some of the Armenian families in the village were given orders to pack up, leave their homes, and march into exile. What could they do? Nothing. If they resisted, they would be whipped and kicked, and put out from their homes by force.

The next day we were surveying nearby Gok-Pinar—a huge spring of water pouring out of the flanks of the mountain, and flowing through the valley toward Hasanbeyli, to supply power to the flour mills and irrigate the orchards and vegetable gardens. Gok-Pinar was the "giver of life." Without it there would be no village and the people of that village loved and cherished it.

It was at noontime that the first caravan of exiles arrived. They sat down at the fountain to eat and take some rest. They opened their bundles, took out the boiled chicken, wrapped it in thin, smooth, and soft bread, and started to eat.

We approached the leader, Giragos agha, a dignified, old patriarch who was surrounded by his family. He offered us some of their food. We hated to refuse it, because it would be considered an insult to his hospitality. For years his home, situated along the road, had been a shelter for all travelers, Armenian and Turk alike. His door had never been closed, day or night. Travelers, mostly strangers, would walk in, satisfy their hunger, sleep overnight, and in the morning, after breakfast, continue their journey. No questions asked, no money requested. These travelers were "God's Envoys." They should be taken care of, his reward he would receive in heaven. That was his belief. That was the belief of all the patriarchs of Armenian well-to-do families.

And now, on the road toward their exile, they were sharing their food with us as their guests.

"Giragos agha, this is awful." I tried to say something for sympathy. "This is terrible. My heart bleeds for you."

"Do not feel that way, my son," he answered. "Great is the Power of Christ. Everything will be all right. Christ is our protector. I have faith in him."

Yes, their faith in Christ, their faith in Christ's power was very deep-rooted; and that faith fortified them to withstand all the miseries that were in store for them in the days to come. "Great is the Power of Christ." This belief, expressed by this old Patriarch of Hasanbeyli, kept them going during all their sufferings.

After half an hour's rest, the caravan received orders from the gendarmes to move on. They got up, said "good-bye" to us, said "good-bye" to the fountain, looked back towards the town where they and their forefathers had lived for centuries, said "good-bye" to it, and then moved on, with tears in their eyes and fire in their hearts.

They left, and we returned to our surveying, but that expression, "Great is the Power of Christ," lingered with me. And anytime a caravan of exiled Armenians passed by with their misery and hardship, I thought about that Great Power of Christ which never manifested itself.

18

The End Of Lebanese Autonomy

On top of the mountain range, a coach was passing. It had to stop and wait because our transit was set at the middle of the road.

I recognized the man inside, Ohannes bey Kuyumjian, the Christian Governor of Lebanon. I went near him and tried to talk to him, but he was suspicious and cautious and preferred to keep silent. He had the sadness of a disappointed statesman.

Lebanon was under Turkish tyranny. The Lebanese had also suffered and had struggled hard, like the Armenians, to have a Christian Governor. It was only one year ago that they had won that right. But, at the first opportunity, the Turkish Government had recalled him and replaced him with a Turk. That was the end of a short-lived Lebanon autonomy.

19

Caravans Of Exiles

We continued our surveying. We had scarcely descended at the foot of the mountain range when the first caravan of Armenian exiles of Cilicia arrived and continued their forced trip toward the desert.

The local government had provided all the means of transportation—horses, carriages and donkeys. The government at first was lenient and careful. They were the inhabitants of Hadjin, famous fighters who had shown a marvelous self-defense during the massacres of Cilicia in 1909. The government was very kind to them and had told them the temporary nature of their exile. They were being treated with kid gloves, because the Turks could not afford any shenanigans, any trouble at a time like this. They were busy on the Caucasian front, in Dardanelles, in the Suez Canal.

The Hadjin Armenians, like the Zeytun Armenians, had believed in the government.

Another week, the caravan of Sis Armenians and then Dortyol, Missis, Adana and all of Cilicia passed.

Caravans were passing day after day, week after week, and we were continuing our job—surveying.

20

The Supreme Head Of The Armenian Church

May 30th

Near Rahjo, as we were completing our work, a covered wagon passed. An old man with a white beard was sleeping inside. I recognized him. He was the Catholicos Khabayan, the Supreme Head of the Armenian Church of Cilicia. He was all alone in the coach. Most of Cilicia Armenians, his flock, had been deported, and the rest soon would be deported. The Turks had ordered him to go to Aleppo. The Supreme Head of the Armenian Church all alone in that coach—sleeping.

But he was not sleeping. How could he sleep when his people were chased out of their homes? His people were trodding the dusty roads toward the desert, toward the unknown. He could not sleep, but the heat in the air, the shaking of the covered wagon, and his old age had made him tired, dazed, half-fainted.

On his face I saw the muscles twitching. They were the signs of the turmoil in his mind for the miserable destiny that his people were forced into—they were the signs of his helplessness.

No, he was not sleeping. His old body was tired, his eyes were closed. He was not sleeping; his mind was wide-awake in agony.

The coach passed. We continued our surveying.

Next day in Rahjo, an Armenian orderly hesitantly approached us and whispered, "Effendi, yesterday Catholicos was here. He wanted to ride the train for Aleppo, but the Commander of the station, a captain, insulted him, chased him away by saying, 'Go away you son of a bitch, go away. I don't want to see your face, you the head of the traitors. Go away. There is no place in the train for you. Get lost. I don't give a damn how you arrive at your destination. Go to hell!' and the old, helpless Catholicos did not open his mouth, did not say a word, and continued his journey in the coach."

Rahjo was the end of our highway. We had finished our surveying. We went to see the Commander of the station to reserve our place on the train for Aleppo.

He was a lousy ignoramus. Actually, a louse was parading on the neck of his uniform.

21

In Aleppo

June 1st, 1915

We arrived in Aleppo and started to plot our surveyings on paper. Zeki Bey, a Turk, was the head of the Public Works Department and he was doing all he could to help us in our work.

It didn't take us long to get acquainted with the Armenians who were my countrymen and were living in that town on business.

Every day, after working hours, we would gather in a house and pool our information. It was in these gatherings that we were informed that in our birthplace, Harput, all the professors, doctors, teachers, and merchants were put in jail and were beaten, tortured, toenails pulled, balls twisted, hung upside down, in order to make them confess crimes they hadn't committed. They were accused of being revolutionaries; enemies of the fatherland, while every one of them were law abiding citizens. They were accused of owning concealed weapons while in their entire life they hadn't possessed even a butcher knife.

The Turks couldn't stand culture. They hated intellectual development and all who possessed or pursued intelligence. They would rather crush those heads if they could get the chance. And now that they had the chance, they were crushing them. We were also informed that those helpless, innocent prisoners couldn't stand the tortures any longer had burned down the jail and most of them were burned to death in the flames.

It had been easier for them to be burned to death in the flames than to be tortured every hour of the day for the guilts that they had not committed.

The weeks were passing, sad and gloomy weeks, weeks of horror. Sebuh, my assistant, had to go back on the road and I had to stay in Aleppo to finish the job. I went with him to the railroad station to bid him goodbye. We were sitting down in the wagon waiting for the trains to pull out.

Aleppo is a flat country and the station was just outside of the city. The Armenian exiles had camped around the station. Exiles that had arrived from every part of Turkey, north, east, and west, to be deported to the south—the desert.

In that field there were no trees, no shade, and the sun was shining over their heads burning hot. The earth under their feet was burning hot. Here and there you could see makeshift tents made out of pieces of bed sheets, carpets, and clothes, to keep away the burning, penetrating rays of the sun.

A sea of humans, as far as your eyes could see, had camped together, surrounded by gendarmes so that nobody could escape.

Who would dare to escape? Where could they escape to? Who would give them asylum?

Anybody who would dare to give them shelter, Christian or Moslem Arabs, would be deported along with his family. That was the strict order of the government.

The Armenians were declared outlaws and they couldn't have the protection of law.

They were doomed. They were over there in that field waiting for their turn to be chased into the desert.

In the wagon was a Turkish officer, sickly looking and pale, a skeleton, who glanced out of the wagon window at that multitude of Armenians and asked, "Who are those people in that field?"

"Armenians," answered another officer who was well dressed and well fed.

"Armenians?" exclaimed the sickly looking one. "Are there still Armenians living in this part of our fatherland? Why have they left them alive? I was quartered in Van when I got sick, they gave me a leave of absence and I am on my way home. In all the towns that I passed through during my travel, Van, Bitlis, Diyarbakir, Mosul and Urfa, I didn't see a single living Armenian. They have killed them all. The serpents, the traitors of the fatherland," he continued, "They should be exterminated. Why have they left those serpents, sons of serpents, alive?"

Sebuh and I were silent, just listening. He didn't know that we also were Armenians—still alive.

It was lucky for us that he didn't know. He was full of hatred, criminally inclined. Millions of Armenians, innocent victims, hadn't satisfied his criminal appetite.

He couldn't bear the sight of an Armenian. He, that pale cadaver of an officer, wanted them all dead, dead by hunger, thirst, misery, filth, fatigue, bullet, axe or rock.

The train whistle blew. I walked out of the wagon. I went directly to the house where my countrymen were gathered and told them all I had heard.

"Not a single Armenian is left in northern, historical Armenia," I said. "Every male has been killed, and every female and child has been forced to travel on the road toward the desert." They listened to the sad news intently and sighed.

Nothing was said, they were silent, but in their hearts there was anger, revenge and despair born out of helplessness.

A whole nation left alone, helpless, at the mercy of a cruel nation, which wouldn't spare the innocent, the sick, the old, the women and the children.

They were silent.

I left the house and went to my room.

22

My Mother And Sister

In the morning on my way to the Public Works Building, I stopped at Dr. Kilijian's home to say "Hello" to him.

"There is a woman upstairs from our birthplace, Harput," the doctor informed me, "go and see her."

I went upstairs. She was lying down in bed and two other women were sitting around her.

"Good morning," I said to her, "How are you?"

"Good morning" she answered to me, stared carefully at my face and suddenly asked me, "Are you the civil engineer, Garabed?"

I was shocked. How on earth did this woman know me? "Yes" I stuttered, "I am."

"Your mother is in Ras-el-Ayn," she continued. "She had received your last letter when she was still in her home, but she didn't have time to answer. They were getting ready for the exile. She knows you are here, so she asked me to look for you and inform you about her."

"How about my sister?" I asked.

"I don't know," she answered.

I didn't ask about my two brothers, twenty and twenty-five years old. I knew they were massacred. No use asking about them. No male of 10 or 12 years had been spared.

I walked out of the house and started running around like a chicken whose head was cut off. First I asked Zeki bey, the Director of the Public Works for help. He was sympathetic, but couldn't help. I asked my German officer-engineer for help. He gave me a letter of recommendation to the Governor of Aleppo. I went to the Governor of Aleppo with the letter of recommendation. The doorman took it in and fifteen minutes later came out with a letter addressed to the German officer-engineer. It read, "the destination of Armenian exiles is decided by the Central Authorities in Constantinople and we, the local governors, can't change it."

I went to the highest military authority in Aleppo—Velee Pasha. He couldn't do anything either, deportation being purely in the jurisdiction of civilian authorities.

Two weeks passed. I was tired and helpless. Every Turk that I knew was sympathetic, but helpless.

Being an officer, I could take the train and go to Ras-el-Ayn and see my mother and try to bring her to Aleppo, but in the meantime, I was an Armenian and Armenians were declared out of law, officer or no officer. I was afraid. A lousy gendarme could grab me in Ras-el-Ayn and send me to the desert to die or get killed.

By the time my military superiors would hear about me and look for me, the hyenas would have feasted on my carcass and my skeleton would be lying on the sands.

My superiors would feel sorry, maybe they would say, "too bad," and maybe they would add, "those cruel, ignorant gendarmes, those bastards," but all that would neither cover my skeleton with flesh nor bring back my life.

I was in despair, in total despair and even I was crying when Dr. Kilijian entered my room and said, "Let us go to the Hotel Baron. A little while ago I was there and was introduced to the Governor of Der-ez-Zor. He seems to be a kind man, let us go and see him and ask about your mother."

I went with the good doctor reluctantly. He introduced me to the Governor. He had long black curly hair, a dignified appearance, poetic eyes, as a matter of fact, he was a poet called Abd-ul-Rezzak.

"I am an officer," I started after I was introduced. "an engineer, building the roads on the Amanos Mountains. My mother and perhaps my sister and my relatives have taken refuge in Res-el-Ain. I am begging from your highness, kindly to have pity and if it pleases your honor, permit them to come to Aleppo."

"Give me their names" he told me, "and I will see what I can do for you." I had the list in my pocket already and I handed it to him. He stuck it in his wallet, which was bulging with all kinds of papers.

I thanked him and parted, thinking about that promise as "another Turkish superficial politeness, smooth and sweet to get rid of me."

He had to leave that same day for Der-ez-Zor. I was thinking, what else could I do to save them on the borderline of the desert? Every hour that passed was taking them closer and closer to death.

Two days later, early in the morning, when I was sleeping in my room, my Armenian friend's son walked into my room, woke me and said, "Your mother and sister and all the rest on the list are in the courtyard of the Armenian Church."

I put on my clothes and in five minutes I was there. My mother was lying down flat on her back, on the cobblestones of the courtyard. She had contracted dysentery and what was left of her was only skin and bones.

Ten minutes later my doctor friend arrived. He transferred her into his home and did everything possible, but the illness had far advanced.

I left the doctor's home and returned to my room.

23

Fatih's Mistake

I entered my room. I didn't cry. How could I cry? The crime was so enormous, so heinous that the tears in my eyes, in the eyes of every Armenian had dried up.

I was thinking silently, and my memory went back to the argument, which I had in the Engineering school with my fellow Turk students who were getting their chauvinistic education from their Tartar leaders in Turk ojaghis (young Turk's clubs).

"All these affairs of the minority races that our government has to deal with is the result of Sultan Fatih's big mistake" they would start arguing. "When he conquered Constantinople he was at the zenith of his power and glory. He could do whatever he pleased and no European nation could interfere."

"In that time, if he had eliminated all the minorities in his empire—Armenians, Albanians, Greeks, Syrians, and Jews, now we wouldn't have those nuisances, the so-called Armenian affair, Greek affair, Lebanese affair, and Albanian affair."

"You are crazy" I would argue back, "Sultan Fatih was a wise man. He knew that the Turks were the fighters, the rulers, the governors, but he also knew well that they are CONSUMERS AND NOT PRODUCERS. He knew very well that there should be people to till the earth, to produce the raw materials and turn those raw materials into manufactured goods. The Turks were not farmers, neither artisans. They were fighters, but the Christians and Jews were the farmers, artisans, and producers and, therefore, the backbone of his empire."

"He was a very wise man. He knew that without the Christian or Jewish productive genius, his fighters couldn't have the ammunition, the provisions essential for the fighters. The minorities, mind you, were the producers, the taxpayers, and the supporters of Fatih's army and Fatih's government.

"Those very facts that you mentioned made the Turks lazy, unproductive, parasites and unskilled laborers" they would argue back. "Yes, we, the Turks, are the ruling nation. We have the Navy, Army, and the Government. We have the upper hand politically, but you, the Christians and the Jews, have the upper hand in industry and trade. Financially, you are rich, well to do. Most of the farmlands, vineyards, gardens, houses, properties, stores, and workshops belong to you, to the minorities. The Turks are depending on you for their living, for their support and for their bare necessities. For six hundred years the Turks didn't have to learn a trade. There are no carpenters, no shoemakers, no merchants, no blacksmiths, no bricklayers, etc., among them. They are parasites and always poor and dependent. If the Christians and Jews were not existent, the Turks, by the urge of necessity, would be forced to learn these trades, would be forced to work in the soil, would be forced to produce, to fabricate, to build. They would be forced to be a productive nation instead of being just consumers, parasites and consequently exposed to your mercy."

"Yes," I would say, "all these affairs are not the fault of Fatih, it is the making of your own government. For example, when your ancestors conquered the Armenians, if they had treated the Armenians generously, righteously, there wouldn't be any Armenian affair. The Armenian affair is the result of the mismanagement, mistreatment, and injustice of your own government.

"The Armenians and Kurds for centuries had lived together peacefully, but when you conquered our fatherland, the first thing your government did was on one side to arm the Kurds, those wild, good for nothing, mountaineers, and on the other side disarm the Armenians. You made those lousy, uneducated mountaineers, those lazy, unproductive Kurds the masters and lords of the working, toiling, producing, taxpaying Armenians. The Armenians, until this very day would work in the fields and produce, pay taxes and the Kurds would come down from their mountains to kill, plunder, rob, kidnap, and confiscate. The Armenians until this very day would ask the protection of the government, but that government, instead of protecting them and punishing the Kurds, on the contrary, would pamper them, feed and feast them. Today, Kurds walk around armed up to their teeth and even kill the Armenians as they please, but if an Armenian, in self-defense, mind you, in self-defense, would kill a Kurd, the government will put him in jail for carrying a concealed weapon and then hang him for killing a man.

"The Armenians never had the protection of the government for their honor, property, and life. It is no wonder that in desperation, mind you, in desperation, they are appealing to the Russian, British, and French governments for help, for the amelioration of their miserable life.

"The Armenian affair, you should admit, is the result of your government's attitude, mismanagement _ _ _.

"No," they would argue, "no, you are wrong." You wanted to be independent, free. You wanted to have your old fatherland, your own king.

"That is a lie," I would shout in anger. "That is a lie. The ones in high government positions are propagating, perpetuating those lies in order to fool you and your ignorant people, and I am sorry that educated fellows like you are fooled also. The Armenians have never asked for independence or for kingdom, not even for princehood. What they are asking for, right at this minute, is the protection of their properties, their honor and their lives. What we Armenians are asking for is that the government should disarm the Kurds, or if they can't do that, they should let the Armenians carry arms and they surely will take care of themselves.

"You have declared," I would go on, "liberty, equality, and fraternity, but we Armenians, are not treated as equals, as brothers, as free people."

Yes, in those days, in our Engineering School, I was considering those arguments about Sultan Fatih's mistake purely academic. I could never realize, in those days that the leaders of Ittihad (party in power) and their followers were intently planning, scheming to rectify Fatih's mistake as soon as the opportunity would present itself.

That opportunity had arrived at last. The Germans were their allies. France, England and Russia were their enemies. They were victorious and their criminal hands were free, nobody could prevent them in their bloody crime to exterminate the Armenian race from Turkey and to eliminate the Armenian affair once and for all.

"We have killed and deported every Armenian in those states where I passed through. Not a single Armenian is living." Thus the words of that sickly looking Turkish officer were ringing in my ears.

Yes, they had corrected Sultan Fatih's mistake.

24

On The Amanos Mountains

Three days later I received orders to return to the Amanos Mountains. The existing primitive roads had very steep slopes and the mules, camels and horses had difficulty in climbing or descending. The road had to be rerouted and it was my bad luck, I was the only engineer on that road who could do it.

I left my dying mother and poor sister in the doctor's home and went back to reroute the road. I didn't ask for a leave of absence. It would be ridiculous, an Armenian mother dying, don't be silly, who would care?

It was in August. I was back on the road again, driving stakes on the slope of Mount Amanos for the construction of the new road. I was sad and gloomy, but working like a horse because I had to. What else could I do? It was a week later that I received a letter from my good friend the doctor informing me that my mother was dead. I didn't cry. I was not even sad. On the contrary, I was glad. Yes, I was very glad, very glad that her sufferings were over.

In the letter he informed me that he had arranged for my sister to be a maid in a Christian Arab family.

On the slope of Mount Amanos, the transit in front of me, road men far away, hatchet men cleaing the bushes, I was directing the picket men to place the pickets for the new road which would carry the road from the top of the mountain to its foot with an easy slope.

I was thinking, "I am an officer and engineer of the Turkish Army, my two young brothers killed, my mother dead in misery, and my sister a maid in a strangers home, and I have to work and work hard, work like a horse."

"One week later fifteen hundred soldier-laborers will arrive to start work. Are you ready?" Colonel Akiah bey, Commander of all the Labor Battalions, was addressing me.

"Yes sir, I am ready," I answered. I was not ready, I was lying. Scarcely the pickets of one tenth of the road were in. I didn't know whether I would be able to carry the road down to the valley or not. It was a chance I had to take. What else could I say? Fifteen hundred laborers couldn't sit down, eat and wait, it was war. I would be branded a traitor, enemy of the country, saboteur, and God knows what else.

Like a flash, the advice of my Belgian professor was ringing in my ear and giving me courage. "There is nothing impossible for an engineer," he used to say. "The only thing about which an engineer should worry is the cost."

Wasn't I an engineer? Therefore, it wouldn't be impossible for me to carry the road from the top of the mountain to the foot. The route that I would choose, maybe, would not be the best or the cheapest, but why should I worry? There wasn't any cost or accounting involved in it. Soldiers working on the road were getting a loaf of bread and three bowls of soup and that was all. Work or no work, they had to eat. Then why should I worry about the cost? The hell with it.

"Yes sir, I am ready," I repeated. "They can start digging as soon as they arrive." They arrived the next day and started digging and I was working feverishly with my transit, inserting pickets in the ground to be ready for the other battalions that would arrive in a week.

Two weeks past, two more battalions. All in all about 5000 laborers were digging, shoveling, blasting the rocks, and breaking the rocks into gravel with hammers. Everything was done with primitive tools, pick and shovel, hammer and wheelbarrow, iron rod and dynamite, and plenty of manpower.

No plans, no contour lines, no map, everything designed and executed on the terrain. Who cares if the curves were not perfect? Who cares if the slope was not smooth? Who cares if the road was not straight as an arrow? I was making the road to follow the natural contours of the terrain, only being careful to keep the slope under six percent. That was good enough for the camels, horses, donkeys, soldiers and horse or ox carts. That is all they cared about. If now and then an auto or a truck would travel on them, oh well, let them be careful. Let them drive slowly on the curves. No sir, I am not going to make a perfect job and be responsible for the delay of the road and be accused of being a traitor, an enemy of the fatherland, a saboteur and then be shot before the sunrise or be sent to the desert to die.

Yes, I had to work hard, work like a horse. I couldn't run away. Run away, where?

Russian or British fighting fronts were thousands of miles away. One hour's absence of mine would be noticed right away. Every bush, every rock would be combed, everybody would be notified, every Turk on the road and every peasant along the road would join in the search. And suppose in spite of all these precautions, I would be able to run out of the country by a miracle.

In that case, all the rest of the Armenian laborers in the battalions would be persecuted, tortured, and sent to the desert on account of my desertion.

For one Armenian engineer's guilt, the Turks would hold responsible every one of the Armenian soldiers. They would start the policy of terror. They would terrorize them all, responsible or not; guilty or not guilty. They would punish them all, chase them all into the desert, starve them, and kill them.

Yes, I even had several chances to kill Enver Pasha, the Minister of War, or Jemal Pasha, the Commander of the Palestine Front.

Now and then they would be traveling in their autos over the road that we were building. We would be notified of their travel days ahead. We would know the exact schedule of their journey. It wouldn't be hard to roll a pine log, or a rock along the road and block it and make their auto come to a halt, then fire a few bullets and kill them from an ambush.

But what good would that do? Instead of Enver or a Jemal, a Kemal or a Nazim would take the job, but just for that killing, the few Armenians whose lives were still spared here and there, would be exterminated overnight. They all would be killed overnight.

That is the way they deal in Turkey. Burn the whole village, the whole town, the whole nation for one guilty or a group of guilties. Terrorize them so horribly that the sight of a gendarme will pass a quiver through their nervous system, so that they will shiver from fear during the day and sweat during the night in their nightmares.

Yes, I was working like a horse, building the road for my nation's enemies, in order that the armies could travel easily, smoothly toward the Palestine front and capture the Suez Canal, toward the Kut-el-Amara, surround the British expeditionary forces and capture 30,000 Gurkhas.

I was helping the massacrers of my family, the exterminators of my nation and the enemies of the allies. I was working and thinking, what could I do for revenge?

There was nothing that I could do, nothing, absolutely nothing. Work and work and work like a horse. I was helpless.

Oh, the terrible life of an Armenian Engineer. Supposing I wouldn't work, supposing I wouldn't drive the stakes in the road, supposing I would stop working, so what? They would get another man, not as competent as I maybe, to do the job, or they would even get a jackass, put a load on its back at the foot of the mountain, make him climb up the hill, put stakes at his footsteps and build the road.

Do not be surprised; it is neither exaggeration nor imagination. The jackass has the instinct of climbing the hill on a very easy slope. In the Orient it is the jackass or the mule that opens all the trails, then those trails are widened by men for ox or horse driven carts.

Yes, I was helpless. I had to work.

25

How I Became A "Yaver"

We were working hard, but were not getting paid. My assistant and I, being Lieutenants, were supposed to get five Turkish pounds per month, quite a nice wage of course, but we were not getting it. For six months we hadn't received a penny. Our own money was all spent and we were living on our Army ration.

Any amount of cash that the battalion would receive for wages, the Major and the Officers, all Turks, would divide amongst themselves and we would always be left holding the bag.

Begging, asking, threatening, was to no avail. "We are sorry, we didn't receive enough cash to suffice for everybody," they would apologize. "Next time, be sure next time, Allah is merciful, you will get your share." And that next time would never come and merciful Allah would never help.

There wasn't anything else to do but to sit down and write a petition to the higher up, the Commander of Labor Battalions, Colonel Akiah Bey. So, I sat down and wrote the following petition:

Most Honorable Colonel Akiah Bey,
Commander of Labor Battalions

It is over six months that we, the undersigned, haven't received a penny for our wages. We can't go on any longer in this condition. Any cash that our battalion gets is divided among the other officers and we are always left out. We are penniless and if this condition continues, there isn't anything left for us to do but take our caravana (dinner pail) and stand in line with the other soldiers for our meals. We don't want to die of hunger. And, if we are forced to do so, it is up to your highness to figure out the consequences of the humiliation and of the degradation of your engineers' prestige amongst the soldiers, your engineers who are supposed to be the technical advisers of the battalions.

Therefore, trusting to your kindheartedness and your sense of justice, we are imploring you to give order to the proper authorities to do what is just and humane.

Respectfully yours,
Garabed and Sebuh

We sent the petition with our orderly to the nearby town where Akiah Bey's headquarter was located. The next day, about noontime, Akiah Bey was on the road riding majestically on his beautiful Arabian stallion. He noticed me and with a stern and angry voice, hollered: "Garabed effendi! Come here right this minute!"

I approached him, stood at attention beside his horse, my hand on my brow and waited for the order.

"Who wrote that petition?" he asked with such an angry voice that I was expecting the horse whip which he was holding in his hand, would descend on my head and crack it.

In a flash thousands of thoughts flashed through my mind, disrespect to the proper authorities and disobedience to the proper channels in sending our petition and perhaps court martial, detention, and jail, anything, anything that the caprice of a Turkish Colonel could dictate for an outlawed Armenian Lieutenant.

"We, Sebuh and I, have written and signed it my commander," I stammered.

"I know how to read and write," he hollered. "I saw your signature. What I want to know is, who put it into writing?"

His eyes were full of anger, my knees were becoming weaker and weaker, and my eyes were getting dimmer and dimmer.

"I, your servant. I put it into writing," I stuttered and waited for the lightning to descend.

"Right at this minute," he ordered, "I appoint you to become my Yaver (Adjutant). Hereafter, you are my assistant."

I couldn't believe my ears. The anger in his eyes had disappeared in a flash and while I was expecting punishment and court martial, I was becoming the Yaver of Akiah Bey, "The Lord and Master of Amanos Mountains" as they had nicknamed him.

The next day he moved his headquarters from the nearby town of Islahiye to Keller where I was living, so that I could be the engineer of the road during the day and his assistant after the working hours.

He moved into the best house left behind by the Armenians and I moved in another one nearby.

Up to that day I was working during the day like a horse. Hereafter, I had to work like a horse and a mule combined, day and night. And was I glad? Yes, I was glad, because I was becoming important, kind of indispensable. From that day on, all the commanding officers of the Labor Battalions changed their attitudes towards me. They all were trying to win my friendship.

In spite of all that, of course, I would never forget that I was an Armenian and to behave very, very carefully.

26
Akiah Bey

Who was this man Akiah Bey that the people, military or civilian, living in the villages and in the towns alongside the road, would tremble, were afraid of his wrath and were nicknaming him as I said before, "The Lord and Master of the Amanos Mountains?"

He was a man of forty years, well educated, athletic type, with piercing eyes, smart as a whistle and brainy. During the Balkan War he had been a Colonel and Chief of the Army Staff, which was fighting against the Greeks in Salonika. Salonika surrounded and put in a helpless position had surrendered to the Greeks without any resistance. Akiah Bey was captured and taken as prisoner of war to Athens, Greece.

After the war he had returned to Constantinople to face court martial, had been dishonorably discharged from service and put into the reserve army. When the world war was declared all the reserve officers were called into active duty to serve behind the fighting lines and thus he had been appointed to become Commander of Labor Battalions.

Jemal Pasha, Commander of the Palestine Army, during that same Balkan War was his equal with the same rank and with the same position, defending Yanina.

Anytime that Akiah Bey would remember that he had to command the Labor Battalions as a Colonel while Jemal Pasha, as a General, was commanding an Army, he would get nervous, restless, unreasonable, and furious.

"Why did I give that decision to surrender Salonika without fighting?" He would tell me, "Yes, I knew that it was a hopeless fight, that we would all be killed, that we would all be starved to death because we did not have enough ammunition, enough food, and there was no hope for outside help. "Yes, it was the most logical, the most humane thing to do, to save the lives of the Turkish soldiers, but the court martial didn't look at it in that way. An Army is created to fight, a soldier has to die. War is not a humanitarian picnic. Kill and get killed, as many as you can. Fight until your last bullet is fired, or your last crumb of bread is eaten. "Yes, I didn't act like a soldier, like an inhuman being. I acted like a man with a conscience and now look at me, look at Jemal Pasha."

He would become madder and madder as he would continue his speech to me, I would be the butt of his anger. He would rave, he would holler. Yes, he even slapped me once or twice, but I never kept any grudge against him in those days or even today, because he was my protector.

"I myself crush my subordinates, but I shall never tolerate anybody to touch the hair on the head of my subordinates," he used to say to me. And he was true to the letter of that statement. Nobody would dare hurt me as long as he was my commander. They all respected me because of him.

Sitting on his right side in his coach, drawn by two beautiful horses, we would climb to the top of the Amanos Mountains and everybody would stand in awe. I could read in the eyes of the Turks the jealousy for the son of a Gavur (infidel).

I could read in the eyes of the Armenian soldier-laborers, the pride for their Armenian Engineer.

But it was fortunate that they, Turk or Armenian, couldn't hear what Akiah Bey was saying to me in that coach. "Be careful," he would admonish, "you've got to be very, very careful. You've got to work hard and work faithfully. No treason, no shenanigans. If and when, any time, I catch you doing something which will hinder the progress of constructing this road, I will tie you on one of those rocks that you are blasting with dynamite and have your body blasted into pieces and thrown all over the mountain slope. Then I will have a report made and have it signed by the majors and captains that the engineer was killed by accident."

I just listened. I didn't utter a word. What could I say? I was one of the outlaws. He could do anything with me, hang, shoot, or blast. But why that "signed report" about the cause of my death? Who cared? Why was he so specific about that report of accidental death? One Armenian dog, more or less, who cared?

That was a mystery to me at that time, and is still a mystery today. Why a report of accidental death?

27

Caravans Of The Deported

The caravans of deported Armenians were passing. I had witnessed the beginning of it when the Armenians from Zeytun were first deported. As I mentioned before, the government at the beginning, provided means for the transportation of the Cilician Armenians, but afterwards Armenians living outside of Cilicia had to provide their own means of transportation. Those who didn't have them, had to walk and carry their scant belongings, their sick, and their children on their backs or their shoulders. It was a miserable sight.

The more the days were passing, the more the misery was growing. Wretched Armenians from Asia Minor, from Pytania were coming and passing. And I, an Armenian, standing alongside of the highway, was watching their parade, their parade of misery. My heart would burn with anguish, I could not help them.

Women, children, sick, old, would drop down on the road, tired, exhausted, hungry, thirsty, and I could not help them. Those miserables who were of my own flesh and blood, I could not help.

How could I help? They were not one or two, they were in the hundreds, thousands. It was not for one day or two. It was for weeks, months. A glass of water, a piece of bread would extend their lives for another few hours or more and then? The death was certain. The death was there with his scythe waiting, sneering, laughing. I could see his teeth. I could hear his laugh and I could even hear him talk to me.

"Go on and help them, I am in no hurry, I can wait, because how far and how long can you help them? They are doomed, they are mine, go on help them, I can wait."

Yes, I have seen my countrymen and women lying down along the road, whining in agony and I have passed by them and didn't help them, because helping them would only mean extending their agony of death. The sooner the scythe of death would cut their lives the better it would be for them.

It was one rainy day that the gendarmes had forced the Armenian exiles, gathered in Osmaniye, to tear down their makeshift tents and start their journey towards the desert.

Those who had tried to resist were kicked by the gendarmes, whipped, hit with the back of their swords, and with the butt of their guns. The caravan had started the trek under the torrential rain. They were soaked to the marrow of their bones and had slept during the night in their wet clothes on the wet muddy ground. And the result—pneumonia and death.

A week passed. Akiah Bey, the Commander of Labor Battalions, had a coded letter from the Military Headquarter in Aleppo. "We are informed that all along the road, Armenian cadavers are spread and rotting. Arrange at once for their burial before they cause an epidemic."

"Sebuh," it was Akiah Bey talking, "I order you to be in charge of those burials. Get all the laborers that you will need with their picks and shovels and start at once tomorrow morning to bury them." Was I glad that I was spared of that heart wrecking job of burying innocent victims of Turkish cruelty.

"We buried fifty-seven of them" Sebuh reported, when he returned. Fifty-seven of them on a twenty-mile stretch. I was silent and in my mind I was repeating the two lines of our most famous Armenian poet:

"If these cruelties are forgotten by our sons and daughters, let all the world curse them forever and ever."

28

The Donkey—The Only Friend

Standing along the road, it was my most heart piercing lot to watch the caravans of all the Armenian exiles. But the one which I saw on a hot summer noon was the most tragic.

A group of women and small children were trodding along slowly on the dusty road under the burning, scorching sun. They were all helpless, tired, covered with dust and sweat, hungry and thirsty. They were forced to walk because two Turkish gendarmes were behind them, pushing them forward with their whips. Not a single male in the entire group was more than ten years old.

The Turks had separated all the adult males after they had come out of their town and carried them away and killed them in the nearby valley. They were from Tomarza, a small town of Caesarea.

Standing on the road and watching their misery, I was asking myself, "Who are the most unfortunate—the adult males who were killed by daggers, hatchets and bullets, but whose agony and misery lasted only a few seconds or a few hours, or these poor helpless women and children condemned to slow torturous, agonizing deaths which will last days, weeks or perhaps months? Their flesh and marrow will melt, their blood will turn white and they will drop down exhausted as a mass of bone and skin and die."

Who are the least fortunate?

They were trodding along with no hope of help from anywhere. Once in a while they would lift their eyes toward the skies, sigh, and pray out loud and I could hear their voices.

"God, oh God, why have you forsaken us into the hands of these cruel, conscienceless creatures? God, oh God, what is our sin that You are punishing us so mercilessly?"

Standing there on the side of the road, I expected the prayers of these poor helpless women to be heard and to see the skies opened, the lightning to strike and kill all the oppressors of this Christian nation. But nothing of this kind happened. The blue sky was intact, the sun was shining more intensely over the heads of these women. The sun was burning and scorching their faces, sweating and evaporating their body moisture. They would ask for water, but they would not get it. No help was coming from men or God. They were all alone.

In the group there were a few donkeys upon which some of the children were riding. Donkeys, the only friends in all the universe, which were with these miserables. Donkeys—their only friends in their hour of misery and agony. The cow, the horse, the cat, the dog, the chicken, all the domestic animals and pets had deserted them, but not the donkey. He was the most faithful and the most trustworthy of them all.

I watched one of them. He stopped, buried his nose in a wet spot in the dust of the road, smelled it, lifted his mud-covered nose to the sky, inhaled again, walked one step forward, stretched his hind legs, and wet over the same spot.

The girl on the donkey became impatient, afraid to be left behind, hit him, kicked and pricked him to continue the journey, but the donkey would not budge. He had to go through his asinine routine to satisfy his asinine curiosity.

The girl was alarmed and started cussing, but to no avail, until he satisfied his whim, and galloping, reached the miserable caravan.

Thus the donkey, the stubborn despised animal of the world, was the only friend of the friendless Armenian exiles in their distress and in their despair.

I remembered my mother in her sick bed, telling me about their journey. "My son, we sold all we could of our household furnishings and with the little money we got for them we bought a donkey so that your sister could ride on it. It was the second day of our journey, when we had scarcely camped, when they surrounded us, separated all the males over twelve, and tied their hands together. They told us that they were taking them to build roads. Your two brothers, Aharon and Levon, were among them. We were left alone, all women and children, at the mercy of the gendarmes. We walked and walked under the burning sun, in the dust, tired and thirsty. Sometime we would stop at marshy water, spread our handkerchiefs over it and suck the water to satisfy our thirst. It is no wonder I contracted this dysentery. The Chetes (bandits) would attack us, rob us, take our money and clothing, and rape our beautiful girls. The Islam peasants would come along and try to take away our beautiful and good-looking women and girls. At first our girls and women would resist, and if they were carried away by force, they would throw themselves down from the rocks, or into the rivers, killing or drowning themselves rather than be confined for life in a harem as the wife of a Mohammedan. But later on, when all their money was spent or stolen, when the hunger and nakedness overpowered them, mothers, in desperation, started selling their own daughters to the Islam peasants to save their lives, and the lives of their daughters.

"My son," she apologized, "don't blame them. You know the Armenian women, how strict they are about their daughter's honor. But hunger, thirst, tiredness, despair and death—slow death, agonizing death—that is different. They were desperate. They had to do something to live. Oh, life is so dear. Nobody wants to die and that is the reason they consented to be sold, to become slaves or wives of the murderers of their husbands, brothers and sons. My son," she would go on, "do not blame them. They were helpless."

How could I blame them? How could any man with a little common sense and conscience blame them?

Yes, standing at the roadside, watching the male-less caravan, tired and helpless, watching the donkey and the little girl riding on its back, I pictured all the other male-less caravans of thousands and hundreds of thousands of Armenian women and children who were living in the cities around Mount Ararat, trodding along roads, tired, helpless, hungry, towards the desert—towards death.

I remembered again that sickly looking lout of an officer in the train at Aleppo, complaining out loud, "Are they still living—those enemies of the fatherland? They have killed them all in the lands where I passed through."

Yes, this group was the little sample of all that cruelty that the Turks had perpetrated in my dear, old historic Armenia.

If and when the dream of all Armenians united and autonomous Armenia, becomes a reality, they should erect a statue of a donkey with an Armenian girl riding on its back. And at the pedestal of that statue, should be the inscription:

"The only friend of the Armenian Nation in her hour of agony, forsaken by God and man."

29

The Cache

On one particular day I was not feeling so well and was lying down on my army cot, all by myself. There was nothing to do, so I was watching one by one all the round poplar rafters, blackened by age and smoke, which were holding up the flat roof covered with branches and earth.

From the rafters my eyes strolled down to the barren walls and started watching all the stones and the mud mortars around them. In order to pass the time, a man in his loneliness, is liable to do anything senseless, foolish and childish. In watching the stones, all of a sudden, my attention was attracted by one particular stone that seemed to me peculiar. The mud mortar around it was kind of loose, and the stone itself was a little bit protracted.

The curiosity got me. I got up, took a little hammer, and knocked at it. It gave a hollow sound and my heart started beating fast, expecting some hidden treasure. I took a table knife and stuck it in the narrow fissure around the stone, and using it as a lever, I forced it out of place.

Easily it came out and fell over the floor, and there, in that cache, standing on its end, was nothing else but an English-Armenian dictionary.

An English-Armenian dictionary in the village of Keller, at the northern foot of the Amanos Mountains, where except the Imam (Islam priest), there wasn't a single Turk who could read or write. Not a single school was in existence for the Turks in all the villages that were scattered all over the mountain range and in the plains on both sides of the mountain range.

It was evident that a young Armenian student from one of the Armenian colleges in Tarsus or in Aintab, when forced to leave his home with his family, his first thought had not been to hide money or treasure, but his dictionary.

They were told at that time their exile would be temporary, just for the duration of the war and he had believed the lie and tried to save his dictionary.

I looked at it for a while and then put it back in the cache very carefully, somewhat piously, as I would do for the relic of a saint. Then I put the stone in its place.

When the war was over in 1918 and some of the Armenians, survived by a miracle, had returned, I often wondered if that young Armenian also did return and find his treasure intact.

That intense was the love for education among Armenians.

Where the Turks didn't have a single school, Armenians not only had primary schools but they had students in every high school and American college.

And that fact, unfortunately, was creating jealousy among the Turks.

The uneducated is always jealous of educated everywhere, that is natural, but an uneducated Turk is both jealous and dangerous, and that is tragic.

30

The Bride

The mountaineers living on and around the Amanos Mountains were not real Turks, but were Turkomen. They were neither Mohammedans, nor Christians. What their ancestral faith was, nobody knew, perhaps an agglomeration of all kinds of superstitions.

For centuries, they had lived a semi-independent life, until some hundred years ago, Dervish Pasha, a ferocious general of Turkish Army, had subdued and forced them to become Mohammedans, but they were Mohammedans in name only. They did not have a place of worship, did not perform "Abdest" (to wash hands and feet before prayer), perform "Namaz" (prayer) or observe "Ramazan" (the holy month of fasting). Their women did not wear the customary Islamic veil to cover their faces. The only things in common with the Mohammedans was their names and their cemeteries.

They did not have schools. Only one man in the whole village, the Imam, could read or write and would perform the ceremonies of marriages and burials as best as he could.

One day, at noontime, as I was resting on the crude bench under the old oak tree, I noted that Zeynab, the oldest woman in the village, was entering the village riding on a horse and behind her was a young woman clinging to her body with both arms. The old woman was as homely as could be. If she would ride a broom instead of the horse, she would be the perfect witch.

The other woman, on the contrary, was as pretty as could be. Her cheeks had the pink and white color of an apple and her big black eyes were two huge magnets.

"Zeynab *Hanem*" (I put an accent on the last word, which means lady), "Good Afternoon. Where have you been, all dolled up like this? You look really charming."

"I was visiting the neighboring town of Islahiye" she answered.

"Who is that young girl riding behind you?" I asked.

"She is not a girl, she is a young widow" she corrected me and added, "I bought her to be the wife of my son, Hassan."

"To be the wife of your son, Hassan?" I asked surprised, "but your son already has a wife."

"Yes, he has a wife, but as you know, she is a little old and sickly. My son needs a healthy, young and strong wife to take care of him, his house and his field."

"She looks healthy, young and strong all right," I said. "I bet you paid a big sum for her, Zeynab *Hanem* (I accented the last word again.)

"Oh, no, effendi, you would be surprised, I only paid three Turkish pounds."

"Three Turkish pounds for a woman like her?" I asked her. I was really surprised.

"Don't be surprised" she interrupted, "if she were a virgin, I would have had to pay at least fifteen pounds, but remember, she is not a girl, she is a widow, but it does not matter, my son does not mind it. I really got a bargain."

"I should say you got a real bargain. I must admit that you are really a shrewd woman. I hope your Hassan and she will be happy."

"Thank you, effendi," she said and drove her horse towards her home where Hassan was waiting to see and greet the girl for the first time.

During all this conversation, the young lady clinging to the old lady was listening to us and was as silent as a sphinx. She was not embarrassed one bit, because on those mountains and most everywhere in the interior parts of Turkey, girls and women are like commodities, sold to the highest bidder.

That is their Fate. (IKBAL)

31

The Bandit Leader And His Dagger

It was evening. We had returned, after a day's work, to our room, and were waiting for our orderly to serve our dinner.

Our dinners were very simple, bulgur pilaf (cracked wheat), or lentils or chickpeas, or the combinations of them, cooked in broth or butter. Once in a long while, we would get rice, beans, or macaroni, mind you once in a long while, maybe once or twice in a year. In those days they were considered delicacies.

That certain evening, I remember well, our meal was pilaf. We had scarcely sat around the dinner table when in walked an Army officer. He was a good looking refined young man who was well dressed and well groomed.

"Merhaba Arkadashlar," (hello comrades) he saluted us.

"Merhaba," we answered him and invited him to share our pilaf.

He didn't refuse. He took a chair and sat down at the table. Mehmed, our orderly, served him a plateful of pilaf and a spoon. He was hungry. These kind of guests were not unexpected. We didn't mind at all this self invitation or "barging in business" of officers.

In that little village, where our labor battalion was quartered in the houses left behind by the exiled

Armenians, there were neither sleeping quarters nor restaurants to accommodate the Army officers.

It was the accepted custom to walk into the house of one of the battalion officers, doctors or engineers and ask for hospitality. And they were never turned away.

They were always carrying an army cot with them that they would unfold, sleep on it during the night, fold it up in the morning, eat their breakfast, thank us, say goodbye, and depart.

After we finished our dinner we sat down to compare notes. We found out that our guest, before the war, was studying mathematics in one of the German universities. I was very good in higher mathematics; therefore, we started talking about that subject. I found out that he was a very brilliant young chap, well educated, had a good brain, and had mastered his subject.

He had a beautiful Kama (dagger) hung on his side. It was about ten inches long with two sharp edges, straight and pointed. The handle and the case of the dagger were silver coated and ornamental, a really beautiful piece of art.

My assistant, an Armenian, who was always as curious as a child, reached for the handle and pulled the dagger out of its case to admire its shape, its sharpness and its beauty.

After he had satisfied his childish curiosity, he handed the dagger to its owner to insert it in the case.

"Oh no, oh no! I won't touch it anymore," our guest shouted angrily and pulled his hand back. "You insert it yourself with your own hand, because when I bought that dagger I swore to Allah that whenever that dagger came out of its case, it would shed Armenian blood, and then enter its case. Oh no, I won't touch it, I have sworn, you put it in yourself," he repeated.

My assistant was as pale as a piece of chalk and I was so angry that I could choke him then and there for his childish, silly curiosity. We were lucky that in that room were present my two Turk assistants and the orderly, or else, who knows, maybe that dagger would shed the blood of two Armenians before it would enter its case.

My assistant, with his hand shaking, stuck the dagger in its case. We learned, later on, from his own lips, that when the war was declared, he had returned from Germany, volunteered and become a Chetehbashi (leader of bandits) that were let out of prisons and organized into groups for only one purpose, to rob and kill the males of the exiled Armenian groups, on the highways, on mountain tops and in the valleys.

He told us himself that he was a 'chetehbashi' and he was not ashamed of it. He was proud of it!

Who in the world could imagine that under that beautiful face and clear skin, in that well educated mathematician, there was hidden a heartless, cruel criminal, a monster that would push his dagger into the abdomens of poor, helpless, and innocent Armenians and pour their insides out?

Who in the world could imagine that a young man would be brazen enough, under his host's roof, at his dinner table, to threaten him because he was an Armenian?

Yes, the appearance, the education, or the clothing can't change the inner man. They cannot change the blood that is running in his veins. To change a cruel man, a cruel nation, into a good natured, loving human being or nation, you have to drain out the blood, the last drop of the criminally inclined blood and instill new blood. And that is impossible.

Changing the cloth, changing the form of government, taking over a new name, to be called "civilized, modern, or democratic," won't change one iota of the man, of the nation of its mentality, of its instinct which are the result of ten centuries of killing and plundering, robbing and raping, persecuting and torturing.

The next morning he ate our breakfast, he even thanked us and said goodbye.

I stood there and looked after him while he rode away and said to myself. "God only knows how many Armenians he and his gang have killed, and now, his mission accomplished, he is going to visit his parents in his own home, to see his brothers and sisters. "Maybe," I thought, "it was he and his gang that killed my two brothers and left their bodies to the hyenas. And to think that I gave him shelter during the night and fed him in the evening and in the morning. I would rather feed him, the dastard, rat poison."

Oh, the lot of an Armenian survivor, nobody will understand, nobody will ever grasp.

32

The Two Lovers

Zaliheh was the only daughter of the widow Hadijeh. She was 19 years old, and possessed a wild and natural beauty that was the product of the pine covered mountain air and crystal clear cool waters.

Although engaged to a beau in the village, a poor farmhand, for almost two years, they could not get married because the custom of the Country was that the boy had to pay to the girl's mother twelve Turkish pounds in gold for the price of the girl.

The days were passing but the boy could not raise the money. How could a farmhand save all that money especially in a time when all the Armenian farmers were exiled and jobs were so scarce?

Although engaged and madly in love, they were not allowed to meet or talk to each other, as that was another custom of the Country. The most they could do was exchange distant glimpses, smile at each other, and maybe wink the eyes.

Any time that the girl had to go out, her mother would accompany her, and if the mother had to go out, she would lock her inside the house. The house was one story, a one room affair, built with dried mud blocks and covered with a flat roof. In one of the four walls was the door and in the roof was a two by two foot square opening through which the daylight could get in and the smoke could pour out. Right under the skylight, dug into the ground, was a little hollow pit, which was the fireplace, used for heating and cooking. Along the four walls were standing the jugs of their provisions. In one corner was the hay piled for their goat. In another corner, the goat was tied. Their bed was spread over the floor. They were poor, extremely poor, and the widow's only hope for a better life was the price for her daughter that the farmhand boy had to pay.

One Saturday, while I was walking along the road, Widow Hadijeh suddenly stopped me and asked, "Did you see the Imam?" (priest) She was very anxious, pale, worried and crying.

"A little while ago, I saw him sitting down under the tree near the village fountain", I answered and added, "Why are you looking for him, and why are you crying?"

"Right now, I don't have time to answer" she said, and ran toward the village fountain.

The next day the news was all over the village. When widow Hadijeh had gone out of the house, she had locked the door and left her daughter inside. The farm boy, hiding behind a tree, had watched her leave. As soon as she disappeared, he climbed over the roof and jumped through the skylight into the house. Hours later, when the widow had returned and unlocked the door, she saw the boy and the girl side by side, sleeping in the bed. Instantly she locked the door and started looking for the Imam to marry them before it was too late.

In a small village like this one, where everybody knows everybody else's life history, if a girl loses her girlhood, and the boy decides not to marry her, she will be disgraced for life and become a public property.

It was no wonder that the widow Hadijeh was worried to death and was running around. She not only sensed that her twelve Turkish gold pounds were vanishing, but her only daughter's future life was also shattering. It is said, "Where there is a will, there is a way." The boy loved the girl and the girl loved the boy. They both had the will and had found the way.

Whether they lived happily ever after, I don't know, because I did not stay long enough in that little village to find out.

I had orders to move to Hasanbeyli for the construction of the military buildings.

33

Chief Of The Code

Quite often, as I have mentioned before, we had overnight guests, mostly military, that would share our meager supper and sleep in our room on their own cots.

This particular night we had a civilian, needless to mention, a Turk, because civilian Armenians had only one way to go—into the desert—and they had to sleep on the grass or on the earth, or on the wet ground, never under a cover.

This one was from Constantinople. He had visited Lebanon and was returning to his home. We were very cautious, very careful. Even my Armenian assistant friend Sebouh, after the dagger incident, was very tight-mouthed.

In a country like Turkey, for any Armenian, it was better to listen than talk to a Turk. If the Armenian told the truth, or ventured his honest opinion, it would be very dangerous because it might hurt their feelings and they could crack his head, if not by acts, at least by words. If he had to tell a lie it was more than dangerous. The Turks would be suspicious and attribute it to ulterior motives. The axiom, "Silence is golden—talking is silver" was never so right for an Armenian. Yes, we would rather listen with a deadpan expression, like a sphinx. Asking questions would only arouse their suspicions and awaken their hates. That was the reason that we would let them do the talking and we would be the attentive listeners.

Most of the time their talk would be boring, tiresome, long-winded, but we would listen to them, as if we were all eyes and ears. In that way, they would feel important, wise and superior.

This guest of ours was not the talkative type. He talked very little, but said plenty.

"There is hunger, famine in Lebanon," he started, "people are dying in the streets like dogs, like flies. So far a hundred thousand of them are dead already."

It was the first time that we heard about the famine and the dying people in Lebanon. It was shocking, but we were used to those kinds of shocks. Our nerves, our feelings, were petrified. Death was not shocking any more. It was all around us, everywhere, on the roads, in the ditches, in the valleys, in the marshes. We were used to it.

We were not getting sentimental anymore, we were not crying. Our tears in our eyes had dried up. That was the reason that very calmly I asked, "Why the famine effendi? Aleppo, the warehouse of Syrian wheat, is so near—almost 'under its nose' as the saying goes. Why the famine?"

"The government," he answered, "created the famine artificially. The government forbade the import of any kind of wheat or cereal from Aleppo, from Antioch, from anywhere."

I did not ask any more questions, because I knew all the answers. Lebanon was overwhelmingly Christian. French political and cultural influence was very strong in that part of Turkey. Its people, civilized and freedom loving, were persecuted by the Turks for the same reasons as the Armenians were.

They wanted some kind of autonomy, for the amelioration of their lot through some kind of self-government, self-determination.

It was in 1914 that with the influence of the French Government, the Turks were forced to appoint a Christian governor, Ohannes Bey Kuyumjian, an Armenian, but the Turks never liked it. They had nursed a secret grudge against them and at the very first opportunity they withdrew all the ameliorations granted. They recalled the Armenian governor and appointed another one instead—a Turk.

I realized at the time, when I saw the recalled governor in the coach on the road on top of the Amanos Mountains, that the promised ameliorations were past history, but I never thought that the Turkish Government would go so far as to create an artificial famine and let them die of hunger in their own homes, on their own sidewalks.

The pattern was the same in Lebanon as it was in Armenia. First: oppression by Turks and the Turkish government against the Christians. Then Christians plead to the same government for amelioration of their lot. Then more oppressions for these "insolences" because the servants shall never dare to ask favors, it is up to the master to grant favor by his magnanimity.

A Turkish government's subject should never protest, because it hurts the dignity of his ruler. The subject should always be thankful for the favors or for the oppressions. The government has the right to massacre the male subjects and then give the widows and the orphans a loaf of black bread and in return it expects them to be thankful for the favor. That is the mentality developed through the centuries in the ruling nation.

A superiority complex that could not tolerate to see their subjects try to free themselves from their inferiority complex, from their inferior situation. They were masters, the others were subjects. They would order, treat them as they pleased, and the others would obey and be grateful. Protests they could not tolerate.

The mistreated subject, in desperation, would ask the help of European Powers. The Powers would mediate and the Turkish masters would give in. But the grudge, the hate, the vengeance in their hearts would accumulate like a dammed river, into a lake. And when the opportunity would present itself, they would tear down the dam and let the torrent of grudge, hate, vengeance, sweep and carry away those subjects who had dared to ask for the amelioration of their lot, who had the audacity to knock at the door of European Powers for help.

The Turks, at the insistence of European Powers, promised amelioration to the Armenians living in northern historical Armenia. They even appointed two Norwegians, Hoff and Westmeneg, as governors, but as soon as the First World War was declared, they were recalled. In the same way they promised amelioration to the Lebanese Christians living in Lebanon. They even appointed a Christian governor, but as soon as the war was declared, they recalled him.

They exterminated the Armenians by chasing them out of their homes and killing them on their way to the desert and now they were trying to exterminate the Lebanese people by starving them in their own homes. In both cases the young Turks were rectifying the error of Sultan Fatih, the Conqueror of Constantinople.

Next morning, after breakfast, when our guest was leaving, he shook hands with us, thanked us and handed me his calling card. I read his title. "Chief of the Code of the Minister of Interior."

"When someday," he said "you return Constantinople, do not forget to honor me by visiting in your servant's humble office."

"We, your servants," we answered "surely will be glad and feel honored to have the luck and the opportunity to visit your Excellency in your most high office."

"Allaha Smarladik" (God be with you).

"Selametler" (Go with peace).

We, two Armenians, unwittingly, had given food and shelter to the right hand man of Talaat Pasha, the Minister of Interior, the butcher and the executioner of the Armenian race—our race.

We had entertained the man whose hand had written all the codes, all the secret correspondences, all the secret orders from the Minister of the Interior to the governors of states to exterminate our own people.

Doubtless, he was sent over to Lebanon to see with his own eyes and witness that the extermination order was carried through to the letter; to see and witness that they were dying like dogs and flies. And this man was inviting us into his office for a return visit. HOW POLITE! HOW THOUGHTFUL!

If the lamb would ever dare to enter the lion's den, then we would dare to enter his office and shake hands with him, when and if we were fortunate enough to return to Constantinople.

34

To Be Or Not To Be A Mohammedan

In 1917 the construction of the road was over and the Labor Battalions had orders to be transferred for the construction of the railroad. Only one battalion was left for the repair work of the road.

There was no need anymore for the presence of Akiah Bey, the Commander of Labor Battalions. He got his order to be transferred to the Taurus Mountains to become a Railroad Construction Supervisor. One evening, a week before his departure, he started talking to me intimately while we were sitting at the desk facing each other.

"Garabed effendi," he started, "I have orders to go to the Taurus Mountains in about a week. I surely would like to take you with me, but I can't do it. To do it I would have to write to the Army Commander Jemal Pasha for permission. I can't do it, because it looks so odd for a man in my position to ask a favor for an Armenian engineer. You realize that?"

"Yes, I realize it," I answered. "It would sound rather unusual."

"But," he continued, "I am afraid for your safety. I am afraid those bastards (he meant the civilian and military authorities) will try to harm you. As long as I was here they wouldn't dare to harm you, but when I am gone you won't have my protection anymore and that will be a different story. I have given serious thought to this matter and I think I have found a way for your safety

"Now, being a well educated man," he continued, "I don't think you believe in Christ to be the Son of God, as I myself do not believe Mohammed to be the Prophet of Allah. That means, both of us have the same faith in common. Christ is not the Son of God and Mohammed is not the Prophet of Allah. Therefore, what difference would it make for you to go from one disbelief into another disbelief? You know what I mean, for your own life's sake you should become a Mohammedan. It is so easy for me to take you to the Imam (Mohammedan priest) in the town of Islahiye, and in five minutes finish the documents of your conversion. What do you think?"

The suggestion was so unexpected, so sudden that I turned pale, my eyes started getting dimmer and my whole body was shaking.

He noticed my agitation and mental condition, the hurricane in my brain. "You don't have to give your definite answer right now," he added, "think it over and give your answer tomorrow evening. Goodnight."

I said, "goodnight" and left his room.

I couldn't sleep. I couldn't think. I was all perplexed. It was a hard thing to answer. It was very hard, almost impossible for me, an Armenian, to make such a decision. It was not a matter of belief or disbelief. It was not a matter of rejection of Christ or the acceptance of Mohammed as your Saviour. It was going far, far beyond that belief or faith. If it were all a matter of belief or faith, it was the easiest thing in the world to repeat after Iman "la-hee-la heh—. There is no other God but Allah and Mohammed his prophet" and even go one step farther and get circumcised.

The belief, the faith, is in man's heart, therefore, why not superficially admit Mohammed as the Prophet, and in your heart admit Christ as your Savior and save your life? NO, IT WAS NOT JUST A MATTER OF BELIEF OR FAITH, IT WAS MY NATIONALITY WHICH WAS INVOLVED IN MY DECISION.

Because as soon as an Armenian denies his Christ, even superficially, and becomes a Mohammedan, he is no longer an Armenian but is a Turk, and therefore is despised, hated, and suspected by all other Armenians.

As the ocean does not hold in its bosom a dead fish but will spew it out to the shore, so the Armenians would throw from their amidst any Armenian that denies his Christ. For Armenians, Christianity and Armenianess are the same thing; an entity, inseparable and indivisible. In all Armenian history there never has existed a Mohammedan-Armenian.

There was still another aspect of the question.

There were quite a few Armenians left working in the Labor Battalions. I was their only hope, their pride, and their consolation. I would read German newspapers, read the war news and if I would find out that the Russian Army had captured Van, Bitlis or Trabizond, I would whisper this news to the Armenian sergeants and they in turn would whisper to the other Armenian soldiers. Thus, the grapevine would operate. They, in their misery, would rejoice. They would be a little happier in hearing that the Turk, their torturer, their nation's exterminator, was defeated or losing territory. At last, God was punishing them. I was their only consolation.

If I should become a Mohammedan, if I should change my name and become an Ali, Hassan, or something like that, all the Armenians would despise me, run away from me and not trust me. I would be like a leper among them. No, I could not do it.

No, I would rather take a chance and remain a Christian and an Armenian and let the authorities harm me, jail me, beat me, chase me into the desert, or kill me, but I won't forsake my poor Armenian soldier-laborers. I am their pride, I am their only source of news that was consoling, giving them strength and hope. I am the only one left to lift their morale.

Who said that I am any better than my brothers, cousins, countrymen, and all the others that got killed or died on the road toward exile in the desert? Who said that I am any better than all the rest that were dragging themselves over the road from Asia Minor, from Cilicia, into the desert of Der-ez-Zor? Who said that I am any better that I should live by becoming a Mohammedan, a Turk? If one million of my people could die, so could I.

I decided to stay a Christian and an Armenian.

Twenty-four hours later Akiah Bey and I were again at the desk facing each other. He did not ask for my answer. He was a wise man. He didn't want to embarrass me, he had sensed it from last night that I would not sink that low.

One week later, he departed.

35

My Sister Alice

Akiah Bey left for Taurus. Major Nuri Bey, an Arab, was appointed in his place. He didn't have the experience for the job, he needed me very badly to advise him and in turn I needed him very badly for his protection. He was very good-natured, an easygoing man, and we were getting along fine. I was glad.

His family lived in Aleppo, and one day he decided to go there and bring his family near him. I asked him if he would do me a favor and bring my sister with him. "Gladly," was his prompt answer "anything for you."

Two weeks later, Major Nuri Bey on his black stallion was leading a covered wagon into the little village of Keller. I was sitting down on the bench under the oak tree, when the Major galloped his horse towards me and hollered out loud, "My reward. Your sister, Ferideh Hanem, is here."

Ferideh Hanem? I was shocked, terrified. Ferideh is a Mohammedan name. Does that mean that my sister had become a Mohammedan? It was terrible.

The Major noticed my upset condition and laughed. "Don't be alarmed," he said. "We had to wrap her in a char-shaf (sheet), cover her face with a thick veil, like my wife and daughter, and give her a Mohammedan name so that in case one of the bastard gendarmes would get inquisitive, we would fool him."

The covered wagon arrived and stopped. My sister, noticing me, jumped out of the wagon and embarrassed me and kissed me. She was only sixteen at that time.

I went over again, in my mind, the ledger of my family. Two brothers in their twenties, massacred. Mother, dead on the road toward the desert. All our properties, confiscated, and now out of a whole family, only one little sister saved, has come to live with me, near me.

That was the ledger of an Armenian officer-engineer in the Turkish Army, building their strategically very important road.

Yet, I was lucky, lucky that I was alive and my sister was alive, because there were thousands of other Armenian officers that were taken out of the regular army and massacred and their whole family wiped out.

I was lucky, comparatively speaking.

36

The Last Goodbye

It was a very hot day. I was sitting on a crude bench under the village oak tree, trying to rest and cool myself. Suddenly, one of the children of the village came running towards me and said, "Effendi, there is a gentleman over there, he wants you to go and see him right away, he wants to talk to you."

I got up and started walking towards the gentleman who was about two hundred yards away. He was hurrying towards me. When we came a little closer to one another, I noticed that he was wearing the uniform of the Turkish Engineering School. As he neared me, he recognized me and shouted "Garo!"

I recognized his voice. He was my Armenian countryman and schoolmate.

"Stepan!" I shouted also and ran towards him. We embraced.

"Are you still alive? What are you doing here?" I asked him.

"Yes, I am still alive," he answered, "but for how long, I do not know. I have lots to tell you, but I do not have the time. I will try to be as brief as possible."

He continued, "There are six of us—prisoners—and three policemen who are watching us very closely. They are taking us to Aleppo. They have a sealed envelope with them, and our fate is in it. Strange as it may seem, we are treated like princes, traveling in phaetons. They are taking care of all our expenses. Why they are treating us like this, we do not know. What is in that envelope, we do not know. You remember, perhaps," he continued, "that I had paid ransom for my military service and I was out of it. So were Dikran and Hacho, but in that infamous night of April 28th when they dragged the three hundred Armenian intellectuals out of their beds and jailed them, Dikran and Hacho were in that group. I went into hiding. You remember that little Tashnagtsagan group that we formed in school?

"Oh, yes, I remember," I replied. "It lasted only three months. We were too busy with our schoolwork to have time for that kind of thing."

"Well, in Hacho's papers they found a record of it plus a snapshot of all five of us. They started looking for the rest. For about eight months I evaded them, but someone informed them and they caught me and put me in jail. They had Yeghia in jail long before me. You are the only one of the five who is still at large. Be careful. They asked us about you, and we told them that you were killed in Dardanelles. They took Dikran and Hacho to Angora with the other three hundred and killed them. Yeghia, after nine months in jail, was set free, and he is now a clerk in a Labor Battalion. That one article of his, published in the Armenian paper against the Tashnagtsagan leader, Shahrigian, saved him. Today, I am alive, but tomorrow...?"

"Stepan," I assured him, "In the state of Cilicia, they do not kill. As a matter of fact, they do not kill even in the state of Aleppo, but after that it is dangerous. Once in Aleppo, try to escape and hide yourself in that big city, because if they ever take you out of Aleppo toward Der-ez-Zor, that will be the end of you."

We finished our conversation because we had already reached the old oak tree where the three policemen were sitting on the crude benches with the other prisoners. They were waiting for us. We talked some more about this and that—about his daughter, about school, and things of that sort. Five minutes more and they rode the phaetons. We shook hands, said goodbye, and they went away.

I heard afterwards that they had safely and comfortably arrived in Aleppo. Four of the six prisoners had managed to "get lost," but Stepan and another could not. They were watched very closely. They were taken toward Der-ez-Zor, but on the road they were killed.

In the Turkish Engineering School we were five young Armenian students from Harput, full of ambition and zeal to graduate, to be somebody. We wanted to be useful to the country by building, constructing, and now three of us were already killed.

When the war was over in 1918, Yeghia and I were still alive. In 1922, Yeghia went to work in the coal mines in Broussa, as an engineer. Kemalists took over the city so suddenly that he could not get out. They killed him too.

Out of five young students I am the only one left to report on them. Four young Armenian engineering students, their lodging, their boarding and education provided for by the Turkish Government, so that they may, in the future, serve their country and help in its progress—and now, all of them killed by the same Turkish Government.

Who can analyze the inner workings of the Turkish mind?

37

Twenty-Four Hours

It was in 1917, I don't remember the month, but I know that the mulberries were just ripe.

The tunnel under the Amanos Mountains was opened. Both ends of the Baghdad-Bahn joined together and the railroad construction was over.

There was no need for the common laborer anymore. All the Armenian exiles who, on their way toward the desert were permitted to stay and work like slaves on railroad construction for a loaf of bread and a bowl of soup, now had the order to pack up and continue their march toward the desert.

It was a tragic sight. All their money spent, all their clothing torn on the railroad work, all their vitality at the lowest ebb, starving, sick, unable to stand on their feet, now they had the order to pack up and move. The railroad was finished. They didn't need slave labor anymore. The slaves should move to their destination—the desert.

The extermination policy had to be carried out. It was only temporarily halted to build the tunnel and the road beds adjoining the tunnel, and now the work finished, they had to move to extermination. The Fatih's mistake had to be corrected.

The road was crossing the railroad at that little village of Keller, where I was stationed. Here in this same town was the Railroad Section Engineers' Headquarters, manned by a Swiss.

Two of my childhood Armenian friends were in charge of the railroad warehouse. Through the grapevine I was informed that the Turkish gendarmes had the list of those Armenians that should be killed as soon as the caravan left Keller, and my friends were heading the list.

They should be saved.

I remember well, it was two o'clock in the afternoon when I rode my horse to Islahiye, where the train station was. I had to see the Aide of Station Commander, a Turkish officer and friend of mine, and ask his assistance to save these two Armenians.

"You know that I would do anything for you if that is in my power, but this is beyond me," he apologized. "The station and every wagon is surrounded and is under the surveillance of civilian authorities. The gendarmes, the policemen, are all over the place. It is next to impossible to put them on any wagon and not to be detected. I am sorry, it is very, very dangerous, it can't be done. Think about some other way to save them," he advised me.

I knew he would do his best if it was possible.

"By the way," he asked me, "where is your sister, Alice?"

"She is in Hasanbeyli, with Manug Kehya's family. You know it is mulberry season and she is there to eat them," I said.

"With Manug Kehya's family?" he exclaimed, and jumped to his feet. "Hurry, don't lose any time, right this minute go to Hasanbeyli and bring her back because Manug Kenya's family is on the list. They are going to be deported tomorrow morning and your sister will be with them. Turn back right this minute."

I turned back to Keller. It was already dark. I stopped at the Railroad Section Engineers' Office to report my mission's failure.

"Never mind your report," he said to me in French. "We don't have time. We have planned with the Battalion Commander working on our railroad to assign one sergeant and two soldiers along with three mules to accompany your friends, Levon and Haigaz, on the pretext of going to far away towns to buy provisions. They've got to sneak out through the cordon of gendarmes during the night as one of our soldier-laborers. We don't have much time to lose. The scheme is planned cleverly, but we've got to have the official papers written in Turkish, signed and stamped on our railroad construction stationery, but at this moment I don't have anybody to do it, my Turkish clerk is on his furlough."

"Sit down at the table and write it at once," he said to me.

I sat down and wrote:

"I, undersigned, am appointing my two employees, who are the bearers of this document, to visit Antioch, Alexandretta and Aleppo in order to buy provisions for the Chilby Labor Battalion, working for the railroad construction."

With this paper in their pocket, Levon and Haigaz rode the mules, and with the sergeant and two soldiers, under the cover of darkness, sneaked out through the cordon that was thrown around Keller.

"Who are you?" the gendarme had asked.

"Soldiers going out after provisions," the sergeant had answered.

"Pass," had ordered the gendarme.

They traveled all during the night, until they had crossed the boundary between the states of Adana and Aleppo.

The authority of Adana gendarmerie extended up to the state boundary.

The sergeant, two soldiers and the mules returned the next day and told us that they were safe.

The night was advancing and I was hurrying to go to Hasanbeyli to save my sister.

"Monsieur Garabed, your work is not finished yet. You have more important, very important work to do," the Section Engineer was addressing me again.

"What is it?" I asked.

"The Commander of Gendarmes, in charge of deportation, has accepted my plea to keep about fifty carpenters, masons, blacksmiths, etc., for the completion of the railroad construction. I have the list ready in French, but the Commander wants it in Turkish and in three copies," he said and added, "it is the lives of fifty Armenian families depending on you."

On one side the lives of fifty Armenian families, poor, neglected, Godforsaken, depending on me and on the other side my sister's life. I took a chance. I sat down at the table and translated the whole list, name, surname, trade, birthplace, age, wife, children, their names, age, etc. It was long past midnight when I finished them and returned to my room and awakened my orderly, a faithful Turk.

"Mehmed, get my horse ready," I asked him.

"In this late hour, what for, effendi?" he was surprised.

"I am going to Hasanbeyli to bring Alice back to Keller."

"Why so soon, effendi, she was supposed to stay with Manug Kehya for two weeks and it is only three days?"

"Mehmed," I answered, "tomorrow morning they are going to exile the rest of the Armenians from Hasanbeyli.

There won't be any Armenian families left in the town and I want to have Alice out of there before it is too late."

"Effendi, it will take three hours from here to Hasanbeyli. It is dangerous during the night over the mountain range, through the pine forest," he advised.

"I know it is dangerous, Mehmed, but danger or no danger I've got to take the chance, I've got to save her. She is the only one left of all my family."

"Allah be with you," he wished me well.

"Allah has forgotten our nation, Mehmed. He doesn't care for us anymore. He doesn't hear all these cries of agony and misery of the old, sick, and the children."

"Effendi, this much zulum (persecution) from our Turks to you Armenians can't go unpunished. I am afraid Effendi, Allah is going to punish us someday, severely, very severely."

"Goodbye Mehmed, pray for me."

"Goodbye effendi, Allah be with you, go in peace."

Mehmed, my orderly, was a Turk, one of the displaced persons of the Balkan War. He was from Adrianapolis in Thrace. He and his family had escaped when the Bulgar Army invaded their hometown. He was scarcely settled with his family when he was drafted. He had tasted all the hardships of a displaced person. He was sympathetic with us, but what could he do?

It was four o'clock in the morning when I arrived at Hasanbeyli. I entered the tent of an Armenian clerk of the army and awakened him.

"Hovannes, is there any commotion today about the deportation of the rest of the Armenians in Hasanbeyli?"

"No, nothing. Everything is normal," he answered.

"Then I can take a nap on this long chair for a couple of hours," I said and stretched out on it.

"Anything wrong?" he asked me.

"You will see in the morning," I answered. "They are going to deport all the Armenian families that for some reason or other were spared so far."

"The cruel beasts will never be satisfied until they exterminate the last vestige of us. They are like the tigers, the more they drink the human blood, the more ferocious they become," he said angrily.

"I came here to take Alice back before it is too late," I said. I laid down and closed my eyes. I couldn't sleep, but just the same I laid there for two hours. At sunrise I went to Manug Kehya's house and knocked at the door. Manug Kehya's wife opened the door, saw me, and her face became as white as a chalk.

"What is wrong?" she asked.

"I came to take Alice back to my room."

"You don't have to tell me, I can guess it. This is our last day in Hasanbeyli, or else you wouldn't come so early to take your sister back," she said. And she added, lifting her eyes to the heaven, "Oh God, what is our sin? Why have you delivered us into the hands of this cruel, infidel nation?"

"Let my sister get prepared," I said. "I will be back in ten minutes."

I went to the Military Commander of the place and asked for his wife's charshaf, veil and a horse. He gladly accommodated me. He was very sympathetic to our misery, but that was all he could do.

My sister, wrapped in a charshaf and her face covered with a heavy veil, we rode out of Hasanbeyli heading for Keller.

A couple of gendarmes that were going to Hasanbeyli met us on the road. They were on their way to carry out their sinister task of kicking out the villagers from their homes that were theirs for centuries.

They looked suspiciously at us, my features being distinctly Armenian, but didn't say anything on account of my military uniform.

We arrived in Keller.

Along the railroad, all the makeshift tents were down, all the huts were empty, not a soul was stirring. The poor derelicts of Armenians were on their way to the desert, to their death.

Their death had been postponed for a year or so in order to finish the approaches of the Amanos Tunnel.

I remembered the answer of the governor of Aleppo. "Their destination is decided in Constantinople and we cannot change it." Their destination was the desert and only temporarily postponed for the emergency work.

Toward their destination—the desert—they were taken by lousy gendarmes who were most happy to fulfill the wishes of their masters with whips and kicks. I have never seen any happier, lousier, good-for-nothings to feel as important and cruel as those Turkish gendarmes.

They would hit their victim with the butt of their guns if he would walk fast in order to make him slow down. They would kick him if he would walk slow to force him to walk faster. Kick and kick.

For four years I saw the Death, with the scythe in his hand, standing in front of me.

Every morning I felt my neck to see if it was still connecting my head to my body.

I was not afraid of death, I was used to facing it, but at the sight of a Turkish gendarme I would shudder. The lousier his whole body, the stinkier his breath, the paler his face, the more I would be afraid and shudder.

The thought of being carried away, tortured and killed by one of those good-for-nothings was passing a shiver through my whole nervous system, through the marrows of my bones.

Oh, that lousy Turkish gendarme, he is still the nightmare of my dreams.

38

The Helpful Germans

The tunnel was completed, the rails were connected, and the trains were running day and night.

All the fifty Armenian families, mentioned before, who were allowed to stay temporarily, on account of their trades, were exiled. Not a single Armenian family was left in all the villages or towns situated on or around Mount Amanos.

I was expecting any day to get orders to move, God knows where. It was very easy for me to move, but what should I do with my sister? I could neither leave her behind all alone, nor take her with me. It was a cold wintry day, I went to the Camp of German Army Truckers who were doing the transportation on the road. I knew their Commander, Lt. Fink. We were friends. Quite often, with my little knowledge of the German language, I helped his soldiers in their dealings with the villagers.

It was a very lucky day for me that the German Schwester, nicknamed Yanuk-Keez by the natives on account of a red birthmark covering the right side of her face, was visiting the Commander. I had heard about her—that she was the head of an Armenian girls' orphanage in the City of Marash. I thought the opportunity had come to ask her about my sister's admittance into her orphanage.

Yanuk-Keez did not hesitate at all. "I am willing to admit her in my orphanage, if you will bring her to Marash." That was a very difficult proposition. Marash was at least 100 miles away and there were no roads, and besides there was a bridge to be crossed which was guarded day and night by the Turkish gendarmes.

It was impossible for me to take her over. Desperately, I looked at the commander for help. He understood my dilemma. "As soon as the rainy weather is over and the fields get hardened so that I can send my first autos to buy provisions, I promise to send your sister with them." Two months later, the Commander kept his promise, and my sister was on her way to Marash. Four days later, the soldiers returned and they had a letter for me from my sister.

"Dearest Brother, I arrived here safely. Schwester Yanuk-Keez is very kind and friendly toward me. I had a very comfortable journey. Once our auto was sunk in a mud hole and the soldiers got out. I thought I also would get out to help them, but they would not let me do so. When we were crossing the bridge, the Turkish Gendarmes stopped us and tried to find out about me. The German soldiers, instead of answering, pointed their guns toward the Gendarmes and crossed the bridge. They were all so wonderful to me. Thank them and reward them. I miss you so much.

With Love,
Your Sister, Alice."

At least, she was in safe hands for the duration of the war.

39

I Tore Down A Church

I was back in Hasanbeyli again, building bathrooms, officer's quarters, bakeries, etc.

One day, the Commander of the Palestine Front, Jemal Pasha, drove by and stopped in front of the local Commanding Officer's building. We were not surprised, as we had been notified three days ago, that he would pass by. However, we did not expect him to stop.

The Commanding Officer, a captain, walked out.

"Captain," ordered Jemal Pasha, "tear down that Armenian Church on top of that hill, transport all the stones down here, and, near that water fountain, build a mosque with these same stones."

"Your command is upon our head, your Excellency. It will be fulfilled at once."

"Continue," ordered Jemal Pasha to his chauffeur. They drove away towards Palestine for the invasion of Egypt.

"You heard, Garabed effendi. The order of Jemal Pasha" the Commanding Officer addressed me. "Therefore, I order you to take some of your soldiers and carry through his command. You can have all the mules and donkeys that we can muster to transport the stones."

"Your order is upon my head," I answered.

It was a sacrilegious job for an Armenian to tear down an Armenian Church, but what could I do? Not to carry out the order, refuse to do the job, and be hung? No, I was not that foolish; they would find somebody else to do the dirty job, but they would not let me live.

I assigned my Mohammedan laborers to do the tearing down of the church. It would also have been too much for the Armenian laborers to tear down an Armenian Church. It would be a disrespectful, a sacreligious job for them to do it. They would be conscience-stricken and miserable for the rest of their lives.

Why should I talk about this one church, while all the other Armenian churches had been torn down or turned into mosques, warehouses, and stables? Why talk about this particular church of Hasanbeyli, when the church of my own birthplace, a masterpiece of architecture, had been destroyed by the Turks with cannon balls?

It is because there is a story behind this church of Hasanbeyli.

When Jemal Pasha was governor of Cilicia, and visiting Hasanbeyli for inspection, he had noticed the church, which the people were building with pure white stones on top of the hill—beautiful, magnificent, and domineering.

"Is that a church or a fortress that these Armenians are building?" he had shouted in a rage, and ordered to tear it down immediately.

The order was carried out.

The Armenian Patriarch in Constantinople, who was the religious head of the Armenian Church, was informed about it, and so were the Armenian Representatives of the Turkish Parliament. A barbaric act of this kind could not be becoming to the young Turks of "Equality, Liberty and Fraternity."

The Armenians were protesting, asking justice for this unjust barbaric act. They voiced their protests in the newspapers and in the Parliament. The Ambassadors of foreign nations heard about it. It could not be considered an honorable and creditable act for the new Regime.

The Turkish Government, to save face, was forced to pay enough money to rebuild the church. And the townspeople started to rebuild the church.

It was a defeat for Jemal Pasha and his prestige. He could not swallow it. The years passed and Jemal Pasha's star rose constantly. He was elevated first to Minister of Public Works, then Minister of the Navy, when the war was declared, he was appointed Commander of the Palestine Army.

Time and again, while he was traveling over this road and passing through Hasanbeyli, he had looked at the church, and remembered his defeat, his loss of prestige. Evidently, he must have argued with himself whether or not to tear down that church again. Was it not undignified for a commander of an army to stoop so low as to tear down a deserted church, when its entire parish was dead in the desert or dying? Wouldn't that be considered a cowardly act?

Now that the Armenian Patriarch was in exile in Baghdad, and Vartkes and Zohrab, the Armenian Representatives in Parliament, had been crushed with rocks on the road towards their exile and nobody would dare to protest, this would indeed be a cowardly thing to do.

He must have argued with himself quite often and for quite a long time, because it was in the third year of the war that he gave the order to tear down the church. The second part of the order, "to build a mosque," was only a poor excuse to conceal his childish act—his small ego— because, if he, the well-known atheist, wanted a mosque for Islam settlers, instead of tearing it down he could have converted that church into a mosque, as his ancestors had done since Aya Sophia. No, he wanted to satisfy his deflated ego.

Thus, I tore down that beautiful church of Hasanbeyli.

40

Scratch The Turk And You Find The Tartar

The Palestine Front was cracked. General Allenby's forces were victorious. The Turkish Army was in a panic, running pell-mell to save its life. Jerusalem, Damascus, Hama, Homs, Beirut, Aleppo were surrendering one after another.

The Turks were desperately worrying about the lot of their Empire. They were worried about themselves, about the responsibilities for their crimes.

This sudden defeat saved the lives of the surviving Armenians who were working on construction or in the workshops.

Pretty soon they signed the Treaty of Mudros. Allied Powers occupied Constantinople, Cilicia, and Asia Minor.

The Armenians still alive returned to their ruined homes and started to lament over their dead, and mend their ruined nests.

Armenian Volunteers in the French Army Legions occupied Cilicia. The Armenians were sure that Cilicia would again be an independent Protectorate of France or England.

My first thought, naturally, was for my birthplace—to find out about my countrymen who could still be alive and living in the village. I wrote a letter to my old friend, Ali effendi. He answered me and sent me a long list of widows and orphans who were living or dragging their lives in misery and terror. There was not a single adult's name on the entire list.

Our correspondence was established again. Armenians from the desert towns, who by miracle, cunning or bribe, were still alive, returned to Adana, the state capital of Cilicia.

The marketplace began to hum again. The phoenix had been resurrected from the ashes. The Armenian Volunteers, in French uniforms, were everywhere. They were our brothers, our protectors and our pride. At last we were liberated, and most of all, we were safe.

The Turks were very careful. They were very quiet, as a matter-of-fact—afraid of revenge. The Armenian Volunteers had not volunteered for the love of France. No! They had volunteered for vengeance for their brothers, fathers, mothers, who had been killed mercilessly, cruelly. Yes. They had volunteered for the REVENGE. The French Army had been only a medium for them to attain their goal.

REVENGE!

But the French Army is not run by revenge. It is run for the political and economical interests of France and France only. Therefore, the Volunteers were treated as soldiers of France and were confined to their barracks, and thus their feelings chained. To make the matters worse, French Army Commanders were trying to woo the Turks who, although defeated, were still a power to be considered. They did not care for the Armenians who were decimated, poor and helpless, downtrodden and neglected and were not a power to be considered.

Power politics was at work again, and power politics is not based on sentiment. It is based on cold fact, cold calculations, cold self-interest. Today's enemy is tomorrow's friend, and vice-versa.

Armenian Volunteers had followed their sentiment—the sentiment of revenge which now they could not satisfy—and they were disappointed! The blood of their race had called them for revenge. They had answered that call but they had been stopped in their forward march by allied politics and intrigues. Their sisters and daughters were still behind the closed doors in the Mohammedan harems, waiting for their liberation, waiting and hoping. The Volunteers were willing, ready, but their hands were chained by army regulations and politics. Their little brothers and their sons were living in Mohammedan tents, herding camels, tending sheep, slaving, and hoping to be liberated. Waiting and hoping.

It was in this kind of vengeful yet restrained feeling, heartbreaking disappointment, and hateful atmosphere that I received the following letter from my friend Ali effendi ...

"Dear Friend:

Do not be surprised. It is almost four years that my son, Hassan is married to an Armenian girl whom you know. She is the daughter of Janig Meguer.

During the deportations, I took her and her mother in my house and protected them. My son fell in love with her, and they got married.

Now, there is an order from the Minister of the Interior that all the Armenian girls, women—married or not—who are in Turkish harems, must be permitted to get out and their marriages nullified.

When I received this order, I called her and explained to her that she is now free to decide whether she would like to stay with us or to leave us. She cried. She doesn't want to leave my son, or the baby who is now two years old and a cute little tot. She loves us, we love her. She wants to stay with us, but we are in a dilemma, an order is an order, we can't go against the order of our government, but there is a way out of it, and that is the reason that I am writing this letter to you and asking for your help. We hear that her father is in the city of Adana. I ask you to see him and explain to him the delicate situation, and get his consent and permission to let her stay with us. If her father consents, the government does not interfere. I repeat, we love her and she loves us. She does not want to be separated from us or from her baby, and we don't want to see her leave us.

Try to do your best.

Your friend,

Ali"

I finished reading the letter. It was unexpected and shocking. So my friend, Ali effendi, the most educated Turk in our village and in the entire state, could not resist the temptation to take advantage of the most miserable situation that the Armenian womanhood was pushed into, namely to force an Armenian girl to deny her faith, become a Mohammedan, marry his son, be confined in his harem, and bear grandchildren for him.

In normal times, this was impossible. The hate accumulated during centuries, and her Christian faith, so profound in her, would not permit any Armenian girl to marry a Turk of her own free will.

Veronica, that was her name, surely I knew her. We were neighbors. She was pretty like an angel—modest, morally pure. She hated the Turks as much as any Armenian girl, but those were not normal times. If they were deported, the next day the Turks would carry her away by force, and her mother would be left alone and she would be placed in a harem, after all, to live with a beast, God only knows how cruel, filthy, and stinky. What could a helpless, godforsaken, poor, feeble,

Armenian girl do? There was not the slightest doubt in my mind that Veronica had married against her will, to save her mother and herself. And now, she had a son, two years old. Yes, a son by a Turk. Yet how can a mother be separated from her son because his father is a Turk? A son is a son. Terrible situation.

I had no doubt that Ali effendi was right in his letter—that she wanted to stay with them. What could an Armenian mother or any other mother do under the circumstances? Thus, cold reasoning was dictating to me that Veronica should stay with them and with her son.

God only knows the immensity of the agonizing life that she had gone through, and now, there was no sense in taking her out of that harem, in separating her from her son, and in making her unfortunate life miserable forever.

How can a mother be happy away from her son?

Cold reasoning was dictating this logical course, but, on the other hand, when a whole nation was massacred, properties confiscated, pretty girls and women taken into harems, into white slavery, when thousands of Armenian young men from the United States, Russia, from everywhere, had left their jobs, volunteered for the single purpose of freeing the Armenian girls and women from harems, the orphans from the orphanages and take revenge for the innocent blood that was shed by the cruel, unmerciful Turks, which Armenian could have the audacity and daring to interfere?

How could I dare to face Janig Meguer and tell him, "Meguer, now listen to reason. The harm is done. There is no sense in adding more misery to your daughter's life. Let her stay with them." How could I face him? He, who in his old age, had volunteered so that he could take the revenge of his daughter. I was sure that if he could get hold of Ali effendi and his son who had disgraced his daughter's honor—his family's honor—he would cut their throats and drink their blood. I was sure that is what he had vowed and sworn when he had volunteered. Do not blame him, nor anyone else. Put yourself in his position. What would you do?

No, I could not talk to Janig Meguer. Yes, he was my countryman, he had even worked for my father. He knew me and loved me, but I could not talk to him because I knew what his answer would be. Not only his answer, but that of all the Armenian volunteers and the whole Armenian nation. I would be crazy to do such a thing. I would be called a traitor, bastard, non-Armenian, devoid of Armenian heart, blood and feeling. They would ostracize me and possibly lynch me.

Now, perhaps you will understand why I sat down and wrote:

"Dear Ali effendi, my friend:

I received your letter. I am sorry to say that is useless to talk to Janig Meguer. This case is not dependent either on him or me. It is a national case, the Armenian national honor is involved.

"The Armenians have decided that no Armenian woman shall stay in a Turkish house. They will liberate every one of them because they are there by force and not by their own free will.

"I wish that six hundred years ago, when your ancestors invaded our country we had not had this religious difference and we could have intermarriages, as the Kurds, Cherkezes, and the Lazes had. Then we would not have been persecuted during these past six hundred years, and exterminated during these last four years.

"For six hundred years, we lived together, side by side as neighbors, but we never intermarried. Sorry to say that you, as a ruling nation, mistreated us and we hated you.

"I wish we had lived together in those six hundred years as friends and not as enemies—not as masters and slaves.

Now it is too late to reason and useless to talk about these things. The harm is done. The hate is there. The abyss that separates our two nations cannot be crossed, neither by my help nor by yours. It is beyond our power. It is not a thing for individuals to settle. It has a national scope. Armenian national honor is involved here. They have resolved that no Armenian girl will be left in your harems.

"Therefore, although it is hard to suggest, the best thing for you to do is to obey the order of your Minister of the Interior and let her go.

"I am sorry that I could not be of any help. I hope I still remain your friend.

With best wishes,

Your friend, Garabed"

Two weeks later I had a letter from him, which consisted of only two lines.

"Garabed effendi:

"It is a shame, that after all these years, I found out that you also, are like the rest of your race.

Ali"

There was no "friend" neither at the beginning nor at the end. A ten year friendship between a Turk and an Armenian had come to an end. When the circumstances had scratched his skin, underneath was found the Tartar.

Now, perhaps you are thinking that I wrote back to Ali effendi and said, "It is a darn shame that after all these years, I found out that you, also, are no different than the rest of your race." No, I did not write. It was useless. I realized that he could not help it. The ancestral blood in his veins had forced him to write it. His ancestors had pushed him to take advantage of a cruel situation. He had forced a helpless Armenian girl to marry his son against her free will. Though he was highly educated and cultured, the Tartar blood was still there in his veins. His culture had been powerless against his ancestral urge. He could not realize his crime, and I could not make him realize it, so what was the use?

It was only a few months later that the Allies could not see eye to eye, could not divide the spoil among themselves.

Kemalist movement started in the interior part of Turkey. Russian Bolsheviks from the north, Allied powers from the south and west, openly or under cover, helped that movement, and that defeated, demoralized, vanquished army of 1918 became confident, powerful, and arrogant in 1920.

The orders from the Minister of Interior in Constantinople were ignored. The state Governors took their orders from Kemal Pasha and Veronica and all the Veronicas remained in the harems to suffer and bear children for their tormentors.

Graduation from Robert College. Garabed is on the left, in the top row.

41

My Sister Alice, Again

I was in Adana when in the fall of 1918 the Turks were defeated. The war was over and the Armenian Volunteers in the French Legion had occupied Cilicia.

One of my Armenian friends had to go to Marash on business. I asked him to bring my sister back to me. Three weeks later, she arrived and we were together again.

I was honorably discharged from the Army and got a job with the Irrigation Works of the state of Adana. We rented a room, set two army cots, spread bedding on them, set the folding table and four chairs that my carpenters had built for me, and started keeping house with the portable sheet metal charcoal oven that my blacksmiths had donated to me.

That one room became our bedroom, dining room and kitchen. It was one year later that the American Missionaries reopened their Girls' Seminary, which was closed for the duration of the war and turned into a hospital.

I paid a full year's tuition for the lodging and boarding of my sister and left for Constantinople to finish my Engineering Course (which had been interrupted for five years) in the Engineering Department of Robert College.

It was in 1920 April, that rumors started circulating fast that the Armenians in Adana were massacred again. I became panicky, fearing that in spite of all my efforts and precautions, I was going to lose my sister.

I went to the Acting President, Mr. Huntington and asked for his help. He phoned to the Bible House and to the American Embassy and got the news that it was not Adana but the city of Marash. He informed me that when the Armenian Volunteers in the French Legion, who were occupying the city had evacuated, the Turks had attacked the Armenians and massacred them. I thanked Mr. Huntington for his help, got out and wired at once to one of my friends in Adana to put my sister on the first boat that was sailing from Mersin, to Constantinople. Two weeks later she arrived, lived three months in one of my friend's homes, and as soon as her passport and visas were all arranged, she sailed for the United States, the land of Freedom.

And thus, I write down the score of my family of five— two brothers massacred, mother dead on the road toward the desert, all the property confiscated.

And I, Officer of Turkish Army, could only save a sister from the Death of the Turks.

42

Magnanimous Bulgars

1922

At Dumlu Pinar, the Turks defeated the Greeks and pushed them into the Mediterranean Sea.

The Armenians, who had just returned and repaired their homes and roofs, packed again and started moving in order to save their lives.

One city after another joined the Kemalist movement. Armenians were trying to get out of Turkey before it was too late. Most of them were caught in the Kemalist net and were exterminated. Some of them managed to get out of Turkey and headed for Greece and Bulgaria.

This is history now, and I do not care to repeat it and bore you. But I would like to tell about a nation, about its chivalry. That nation is the Bulgarian nation.

I was the first Armenian who got out of Constantinople and went to Bulgaria. This time I did not want to be caught in the net as before.

The year before, I was working for Socony on their construction work in the city of Burgas in Bulgaria. After I had graduated from Robert College's Engineering School, my teachers had procured this job for me. After the work was completed, I returned to Constantinople with a round trip passport. That passport came in handy. When everybody was struggling for passports and visas, and were ready to pay enormous sums of money for them, it became a routine matter for me to go to the Bulgarian Consulate, pay the regular fee and get my return visa. One night I took the boat, at six o'clock on Sunday morning I was in Burgas, Bulgaria.

Two weeks later the Armenian refugees were at the Bulgarian border. The Turks were at their heels. In a few days the Turkish Yatagan would reach and cut their throats. Armenian notables in Sofia, capital of Bulgaria, begged the Bulgarian government to open their borders and let the Armenians enter the country and be spared from certain annihilation. The Bulgarian government, the Agrarian Party's government, opened the border and a torrent of Armenian refugees poured in.

What is so magnanimous about this, you may ask me? Bear with me and let me explain. First, Bulgaria in that World War I, was on the side of Axis; that is on the side of the Germans and Turks. Armenian sympathy, on the contrary, was with the Allies, that is with Russia, France and England. They, Armenians, had participated in the war with volunteers, both in Russian and French Armies. That means that Bulgarians and Armenians had fought against each other.

At the Palestine Front, in General Allenby's Army, that army that cracked the Turkish Army's backbone, Armenian Volunteers had fought valiantly and pushed the Turks back from the hill of Arara. Allenby had commented then on their bravery, for their share in the victory. Bulgaria was aware of this fact.

Secondly, Bulgars being a defeated nation, had lost territory to Greece, Serbia, and Romania. The Bulgars from these lost countries had taken refuge in Bulgaria and were quartered in old railroad wagons and empty warehouses.

Third, the Allies had imposed on Bulgaria huge war fines, the result of which was that the Bulgar people were taxed heavily in order to meet those payments.

Fourth, they had their own widows, their own orphans, and maimed soldiers, the result of three wars in six years time, and those people required care.

In spite of all these handicaps, the peasants' government agreed to open the frontiers if the Armenians would promise: first, to keep out of five thickly populated cities—Rusjuk, Varna, Bourgas, Phillippopolis and Sofia. Second, not to expect any help from the Government or from charitable institutions.

Armenian notables promised and signed. The frontiers were thrown open. The Armenian refugees poured into the country and headed toward those five forbidden cities—18,000 of them. Most of them were just married couples, the women were pregnant, they went to Bulgar hospitals to bear children and none were refused.

Armenians, as soon as they put their feet on Bulgarian soil, did not keep their promises. The Bulgarian Government was aware of it, but were lenient. They were hospitable and lenient in spite of the fact that we had been in their enemies' camp, because only fifty years ago they, being under the Turkish tyranny, understood well the tragic lot of the Armenians.

If they had refused to open the gates of their country, today 18,000 Armenian skeletons would cover the fields of Tartar Pazarjik.

We are grateful to the Bulgars for their hospitality, for their magnanimous deed, for their leniency.

43

Men Or Mice?

Many times, in the United States, I am asked, "How come one Turkish gendarme could carry a flock of Armenians to the desert? Why wouldn't they kill him and run away?"

My answer has always been, "How come a couple of masked bandits walk into a store, in a bank or in a bar, and order everybody in the place to line up along the wall, lower their pants down, lift their hands up, get robbed and nobody dares to kill the bandits? Because the bandits have the loaded gun and the crowd has none."

Yes, that was the case with the Armenians.

The Turks had the Army and the Navy. Every Turkish home was an arsenal of all kinds of weapons but for the Armenians it was forbidden to have in their possession a knife longer than six inches.

Any Armenian who dared to conceal a gun in his home and it was discovered in a sudden, unexpected raid by the gendarmes, was put behind bars, given the third degree, and if he was strong enough to endure and not die, he was put in the dungeon for life.

Such was the Armenian lot. But in spite of all these odds against them, the Armenians resisted in quite a few places.

The heroic Armenians of Shabin-Kara-Hisar, the night before deportation, barricaded themselves in that city's old fortress built on top of the hill, and resisted for thirty days, until their ammunition was exhausted and the fighting youth, against their will, obeyed their mother's and wive's plea, shouldered their empty guns, dispersed and hid themselves in the woods and caves and turned into bandits all during the war.

The rest surrendered, the old males were massacred and the females deported.

Edessa, another city in the south, barricaded themselves in their churches, in their streets, fabricated their own powder, bullets, and resisted for weeks.

But, at the end they also suffered the same sad and tragic fate.

The five towns of Musa Dagh, along the Mediterranean Sea, gathered round the summit of their rocky mountains, resisted for forty days, until the French Cruiser which was roaming in the waters, was notified and they were taken aboard and saved.

Van, another big city, near the Russian border, resisted successfully for twenty-five days, until the Russian Army in his advance, occupied the city and the Armenians were saved.

Yes, the Armenians were not mice, they were men. When the Russian Army in its victory was demoralized by the Communist propaganda, and the soldiers left the front lines and ran back to their homes, the Armenians were left all alone to defend the Russian Frontier against the Turkish Army, and they did it valiantly. They stopped the Turks in their tracks and saved Caucasia.

Yes, when the Armenians had equal chances they proved that they were not mice, but men. Brave men, valiant fighters.

44

In The Land Of Four Freedoms

I waited for a whole year in Bulgaria, waiting for the political situation to clear, so that Socony could continue its construction activities again.

I received a letter from my chief engineer, Aggiman, who was in Constantinople. "Why are you wasting your time and savings? God only knows when the political situation will clear up. Go to the United States."

I followed his advice and took a boat and landed in New York on December 3, 1923.

In the office where I am working, I once remarked, "I am a better citizen than anyone of you fellows." They didn't understand what I meant, and some of them felt insulted. One of them even became furious that he was going to sock me.

"Yes," I repeated, "I am a better citizen than most of you people who have been born in the United States.

"I mean, that I appreciate it more than any one of you fellows, because you are like the sons of rich people, that are born with the silver spoon in their mouth and have never felt poverty and want, therefore never appreciate their wealth and their comfort.

"You are born in democracy, you are born in freedom, you have never lived under despotism or slavery.

"You talk about the Four Freedoms—Freedom of Speech, Freedom of Belief, Freedom of Press, and Freedom of Want—but they are all words and phrases for you without depth in them, but for me they have depth, and they have meaning."

"For years, in my birth place, I could not say what I thought or what I believed.

"For years I could not write what I thought, because if I had done so I would have been dragged out of my bed at night and put behind the bars, tortured, and possibly hanged.

"For years I lived a life of terror, always careful about what I said. I would look around me before I would open my mouth, in order to see if a stranger was listening in.

"For four years I was in a perpetual terror for my life. Every morning and evening I was feeling my neck with my hands to see if it was still there connecting my head to my body.

"For four years I served in their army, built roads, strategically important roads, while they were dragging my family out of their home, killing my two brothers, confiscating all of my property, expelling my old mother and young sister to the desert to starve and die.

"Surely I am a better citizen. I mean, I appreciate this country better than any one of you fellows who served for your country in the wars. The government took care of your families when you were fighting and when you came back; you had the G.I. Bill of Rights waiting for you. You are taking all these for granted, and pardon me; I even have my doubts whether or not you are fully appreciating them.

"Happiness can be a negative feeling. You should be hungry to appreciate food, you should be thirsty to appreciate water, and you should be persecuted to appreciate democracy and freedom.

"In order to appreciate something, you should have wanted and really wanted it.

"You are born in a democracy, in abundance, and you don't know it. Worse yet, you don't know that you don't know it, but I know it and I appreciate that democracy, that abundance more than you do.

"A piece of stale bread and a kernel of garlic was a feast for Armenians in the desert, but for you it is disgusting and despicable.

"I and my fellow Armenians who came out of that Jehennem and found asylum in this paradise of yours, we surely appreciate its beauty, its freedoms, its real Equality, Fraternity, Democracy, Justice and Liberty for all.

"We appreciate the fact that our votes are just as good as yours in order to elect the president of this, our United States.

"Now, I hope you understand why I am a better citizen."

Eulogy

Garabed Hagop Aaronian (Aharonian)

Marriage of Garabed and Perouze Aaronian in Marseille, France, in June 1929.

Our dear father, Garabed Hagop Aaronian, passed away on May 3, 1983, following a lengthy illness. He was born on March 20, 1886, in the village of Husenik, in Kharpert, Turkey.

Garabed was the third of six sons and two daughters born to Altoon and Hagop Aaronian. Two of his brothers, Aharon and Levon, died in the Turkish massacre of World War I, his brothers Apel, Nishan and Krikor and a sister, Maritza all preceded him in death.

As with other Armenians of the time, he witnessed many atrocities.

Garabed, or Garo, as he was affectionately known among his many friends, attended the Medresseh Turkish Primary School in Husenik and Euphrates College which was established by American missionaries. Following graduation, he taught school for a time in his hometown.

Later, he attended Robert College in Istanbul, Turkey, with the aid of a scholarship. After more than three years of college, on February 21, 1915 he was drafted into the Turkish Army and was sent to Mount Amanos in Cilicia to work as an Engineer-Officer and as Adjutant to Akiah Bey, being directly responsible for the construction of roads that had to pass over the mountain range. The famous Berlin-Baghdad Bahn (Railroad) from either side had reached to the mountain range, but had stopped before being joined and completed. In the Fall of 1918, after a five-year interruption, he returned to Robert College to finish his Engineering Courses, finally graduating from its School of Engineering in 1920.

While in Aleppo, Syria, where a surveying project had ended, he heard that his mother, one of his sisters, and a number of others were trapped in the village of Res-El-Ain and faced inevitable doom. Following much resistance in his pleas for assistance, he eventually was fortunate enough to obtain the aid of the Governor of Der-ez-Zor who asked for the names of all the individuals and said he would see what he could do. Two days later, Garabed was informed that they had all been spared and had arrived in Aleppo— only to find that his mother was at death's door. She passed away one week later. All the twenty or more others, however, were saved!

Following his discharge from the service and his graduation from Robert College, Robert College procured a position for him in Sofia, Bulgaria, working for Socony Oil, where he remained for a time.

He immigrated to his dreamland, the United States of America, in 1923, and initially settled in Providence, Rhode Island, where his eldest brother Apel and family resided.

In 1929 he journeyed from Providence to Marseille, France, where he proposed to and married Perouze, a young lady he knew before, who was the daughter of Lucia and Garabed Parsekian.

He brought his bride back to the United States and settled in Pittsburgh, Pennsylvania, where he worked for Bethlehem Steel. There they were blessed with the birth of their son, Dr. James B. Aaronian.

In 1933, they moved to Youngstown, Ohio, where he worked for Truscon Steel. It was there that their other child, Arlene Aaronian, was born in 1936 and, shortly thereafter, due to the depressive state of the economy, the family was forced to once again relocate to Highland Park, Michigan, where Garo was happily employed by the firm Griffels and Vallet as a Civil Engineer for 18 years.

Finally in September 1954, a long time dream was consummated. The Aaronian family relocated itself to California, taking up permanent residence in Altadena.

Up until Mr. Aaronian's retirement in 1958 at the age of 72, he was employed by the firms of Holmes & Narver and The Ralph M. Parsons Company.

Garabed Aaronian may be remembered by the older Armenians as he wrote articles for approximately 45 years in both the Hairenik and the Asbarez newspapers.

In 1955, a hardback book he wrote in Armenian pertaining to his hometown, Husenik, was published. Additionally, he thoroughly researched and made his family tree going back nine generations.

Mr. Garabed Aaronian is survived by his two children, Dr. James B. Aaronian and Arlene J. Aaronian, and one grandson, Dr. Matthew Aaronian.

He was devout in his religious studies, habits and application of our Lord's teachings in his everyday life. His considerate and caring ways toward all ages, whether little children who he adored, or his peers, attest to the gentle nature he possessed throughout his lifetime.

He was an extremely conscientious and hard working person—a man of high morals and principles. He possessed only kindness in his heart. He was strong, but humble, a man of great dignity to the end, more concerned with the health and well-being of others than his own immediate condition. He possessed a will to live that was amazing, yet vitalizing, for those around him.